TEA SHOP WALKS
IN THE COTSWOLDS

Norman & June Buckley

Published by Sigma Leisure – an imprint of
Sigma Press, 1 South Oak Lane, Wilmslow, Cheshire SK9 6AR, England.

British Library Cataloguing in Publication Data
A CIP record for this book is available from the British Library.

ISBN: 1-85058-562-8

Typesetting and Design by: Sigma Press, Wilmslow, Cheshire.

Printed by: MFP Design & Print

Cover photograph: Tea Room at Snowshill Manor *(June Buckley)*

Maps: Jeremy Semmens

Photographs: the authors

Disclaimer: the information in this book is given in good faith and is believed to be correct at the time of publication. No responsibility is accepted by either the author or publisher for errors or omissions, or for any loss or injury howsoever caused. Only you can judge your own fitness, competence and experience.

Preface

The concept of combining a good walk with the refreshment offered by a teashop is now well established in this series of books. Of course, both walk and teashop have to be carefully selected. For the great majority of users of the guides, a walk should be primarily in attractive and, if possible, well-varied countryside. There should be good views and interesting features along the way, including villages and, preferably, historic towns.

To ensure accessibility to the widest possible range of walkers, mileages should be short to moderate, ascents not too prolonged, and any potential difficulties such as severe scrambling should be avoided. From an initial summary it should be possible to assess each walk at a glance. "Rambling" is probably a fair description of the kind of walking which combines so well with the tea shop.

The relaxation and refreshment provided by a suitable tea shop is perfectly complementary to such a walk. The first requirement is that walkers must be welcome, even though the removal of muddy boots may, not unreasonably, be requested. Although the basic minimum is the provision of pots or cups of tea, coffee, and cold drinks, the great majority provide more – usually much more, with cakes, scones, and often light cooked meals. In each case, details are given in the description.

As those familiar with this series of books will already know, in the quest for suitable tea shops, many types of establishment are examined and one of the attractions is the rich variety including, for example, garden centres and premises operated by the National Trust and the Forestry Commission among those deemed to be worthy of inclusion. It has to be accepted that the opening hours of tea shops, particularly out of season, will sometimes change at short notice, often in accordance with the weather, and that the information given in the book, whilst accurate at the time, may be varied. For this reason, telephone numbers are given.

Having set out what seem to be the fundamental requirements for the combination of walk and tea shop, it follows that some areas of the country will lend themselves to this format much better than others. In this respect, few districts can compete with the Cotswolds, where the rolling countryside, the long views, the beautiful villages and historic towns, rich in tea shops, all combine to provide the ideal blend of walks and refreshments.

As can be seen from the key map, the twenty-eight walks in this book provide good coverage of this outstanding area, with particular concentration along the western and northern scarps, where the most spectacular countryside is to be found. More centrally, the immensly popular towns and villages, such as Cirencester, Stow-on-the-Wold, Moreton-in-Marsh, Bourton-on-the-Water, Burford and the Slaughters, with the associated quiet, gentle, valleys of the rivers Leach, Windrush and Coln, are by no means neglected.

Towns, villages, and tourist attractions associated with each walk are described and advice is given on car parking. In a popular visitor area such as the Cotswolds, there is obvious environmental advantage in using public transport where this is possible and reasonably convenient. Alas, railway services are few and far between. The Oxford to Worcester and the Swindon to Cheltenham and Gloucester lines cross the area, with possibly useful stations at Shipton-under-Wychwood, Kingham (for Bleddington), Moreton-in-Marsh, Kemble, Stroud, Cheltenham and Gloucester. Bus services are much more widespread; a special leisure bus (no.166) operates on Sundays and Bank Holidays from late May to Late September, serving the northern fringe of the district, including Winchcombe, Toddington, Stanway, Stanton, Broadway, Chipping Camden, and Mickleton, with links to Tewkesbury, Worcester, Evesham and Stratford-upon-Avon.

Norman & June Buckley

Contents

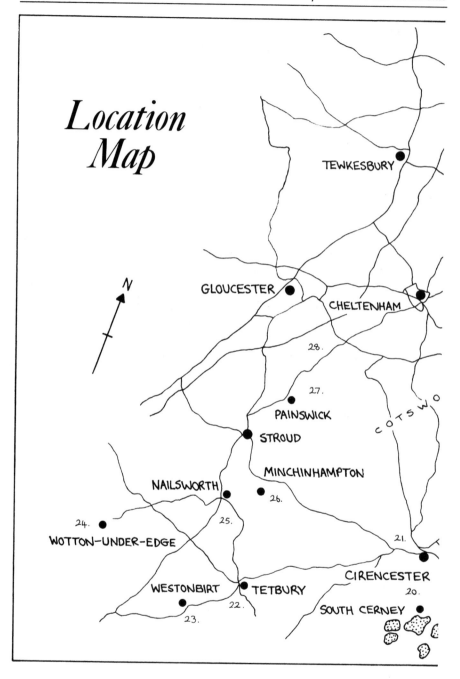

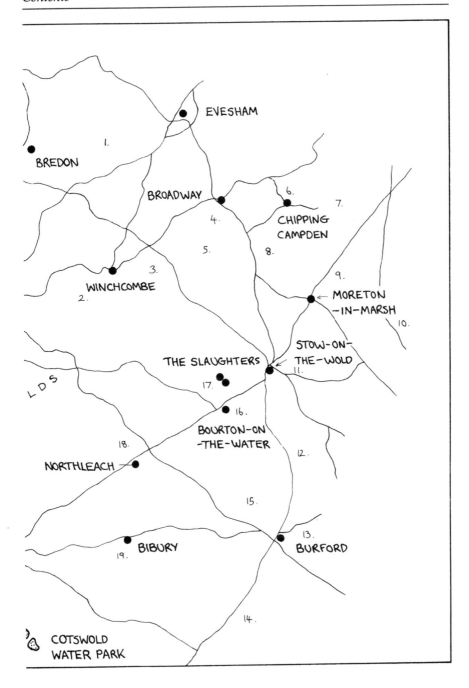

Introduction

Character

Most people would agree that the Cotswold area has a certain character which differentiates it from anywhere else in the United Kingdom. We all know when we are in the Cotswolds. Asked to define the essential elements of this claimed uniqueness, however, many of us might well be hard pressed.

The "Wold" or plateau areas are certainly a major feature but are by no means unique or, indeed, particularly attractive. The river valleys which bisect them, whilst undoubtedly pleasant, are by no means of such landscape significance as, say, those of the Peak District of Derbyshire. No parts of the plateau are shaped into well-formed hills, let alone real peaks so, on the whole, with the notable exception of the scarp to the north and west, the landscape is pleasant without being in any way outstanding.

When we consider present evidence of human settlement of the district in relation to the landscape, we are on firmer ground. It could be claimed that the small towns and villages of the Cotswolds are not only unlike those anywhere else but are, in fact, the crowning glory of the area. Other parts of Britain do have villages built in locally quarried stone, attractively grouped, nestling by streams along valley bottoms or perched part way up gentle hillsides, but in no other area is this a feature of such widespread attraction. Likewise, nationally, there are plenty of small, historic towns, but the consistency of style which the wool trade and its attendant wealth has brought to the smaller Cotswold towns does contribute very significantly to this rather elusive "character".

Add the rich evidence of older human occupation, such as the Neolithic long barrows, the great arc of iron age hill forts along the crest of the scarp, and some of the finest remains of Roman villas in the land, and the "unique area" claim becomes unassailable.

Geography and Geology

There seems to be wide disagreement on the geographical area which actually constitutes "the Cotswolds" and on where boundaries should be drawn, particularly in the east. Originally the term was applied only to the plateau (wold) area adjacent to Stroud, but there has long been generally accepted use of the term to include a much greater area. So far as the landscape is concerned, the long scarp provides good definition to most of the north and west, subject to a question mark over Bredon Hill in the former case. In the south the area is often defined by reference to the main railway line or, latterly, the M4 motorway, although the high ground running down well to the south of these lines, almost to Bath, is included in some guides. It does not, of course, really matter. In this book the spread of walks keeps broadly within generally accepted Cotswold country, concentrating on the more attractive countryside, the finest towns and villages, and the recommended tea shops.

In geological terms the area is a part of the great belt of oolitic limestone stretching from Dorset to Yorkshire laid down under the sea 170 to 100 million years ago. The Cotswolds form the widest part of this belt, with a raised plateau at 400 to 800 feet altitude tilting from west to east. Because the oolitic limestone is less readily dissolved in water than the carboniferous limestone of, say, the Mendips, cave systems and gorges are absent and the river valleys are comparatively wide and shallow. Those flowing west, such as the River Frome, to join the River Severn, are much steeper and faster running than the more leisurely rivers such as the Coln, Leach, Windrush, and Evenlode, which all flow roughly south east to join the River Thames. The otherwise generally straight line of the scarp has been convoluted around Stroud and Nailsworth by the cutting of the Frome and its tributaries, producing landscape of high quality.

Human Occupation

Several stone age villages have been identified and are being excavated from time to time to supplement knowledge gained so far from the fine long barrows but, apart from the clusters of tumuli, evidence of their bronze age successors is sparse. No less than seventeen iron age hill forts, ranging from 3 to 100 acres in extent, have been identified along the crest of the scarp, dating from about 600 BC onwards. Roman occupation was clearly extensive, producing substantial farming estates based on villas such as that at Chedworth, arguably the finest in Britain. Cirencester became, after London, the second city of England, at the junction of several important roads which still to some extent determine the routes of the great Cotswold highways. The Fosse Way is the most obvious example.

The two human activities which have had, and which continue to have, the most impact on the Cotswolds as we see them today are, firstly, stone quarrying and, secondly, the farming of sheep with the subsequent processing of the wool. The limestone has long proved to be a first class building material, resulting in the development of many quarries, large and small, and the construction of the towns and villages which are so admired and which, as already argued, contribute so much to the character of the area. Sheep farming, with the superimposition of the dry stone walls during the land enclosures carried out between 1700 and 1840, has shaped the landscape, whilst the water-powered mills provided for the fulling and weaving processes became the industrial backbone from early times. This woollen industry has had distinct phases, the medieval when it was largely an export trade, dominated by merchants of enormous wealth who promoted the growth of towns such as Northleach and Chipping Camden. The great "woollen churches" which these merchants financed are perhaps the most important surviving single feature of this period of Cotswold history. Later, exports declined as cloth making grew. Advancing technology, improved transport, and the benefits of scale inevitably concentrated much of the industry in the valleys around Stroud, factories being constructed alongside the faster, more potent, water power of that area, later followed by the steam power of the industrial revolution.

In more recent times profitable arable crops have largely superseded the sheep on much of the uplands, the top of Bredon Hill being a notable example. However, large areas, particularly on the steep and difficult slopes of the scarp, remain covered by woodland, traditional trees such as beech, oak, and ash being common, adding much to the diversity and attraction of the landscape. Unimproved "common" grassland is fairly rare, the only areas of note being at Cleeve Hill and Minchinhampton, both included in walks in this book. Gravel extraction, resulting in the flooded pits of the Cotswold Water Park, has produced a quite different landscape in the south east corner of the district where the plateau has dipped to its lowest level, more attractive than might be expected.

Fortunately, the growth of most of the towns and villages has been slow and has remained generally consistent with the character established in medieval times. Largely because the material of the structures, even the thinly cut stone of the roofs has been wrested from the nearby ground and styles have changed little over a long period of time, there is a wonderful degree of blending with the landscape. Local stone, with variations in colour from gold, through honey, to grey and almost off-white, gives subtle distinction to each town and village. With all the obvious advantages, it is not surprising that from very early times the Cotswolds have attracted members of the nobility and other wealthy people to construct castles and manor houses surrounded by large areas of parkland, which have become a well-established feature of the landscape.

Walking

Looking at the blend of landscape, human activity, and history, it becomes quite obvious why the area has long been one of the finest in Britain for country walking, generally of the gentler type, recognising that the small towns and villages play an important part in the enjoyment of most walks. Not that the walking is by any means all of Sunday stroll standard. Some long distance routes, most notably the Cotswold Way, can involve some long days of quite hard walking with a fair amount of up and down.

The Cotswold Way, of about 100 miles, is a well-conceived and organised continuous route which includes a good proportion of the best Cotswold countryside. There any many, perhaps too many, other designated routes, many of them seeming to be rather contrived and having very little historic or other significance. The area covered by this book includes parts of the Cotswold Way, Heart of England Way, Wychwood Way, Wardens Way, D'Arcy Dalton Way, and the Oxfordshire Way. All contribute some of their length to one or more of the walks in the book. Indeed, one or two of the walks include small parts of two or more of these designated routes within quite a modest total distance.

1. Bredon Hill

Length: 7½ miles

Summary: A good upland tramp over the distinctive isolated mound of Bredon Hill, starting and finishing at the village of Ashton under Hill. There is a fairly long ascent at the start of the walk but the gradients are reasonable and there is no problem underfoot. The route visits the hamlets of Conderton and Grafton.

Car Parking: There is no official car park in Ashton under Hill, so find the best possible roadside space, not too far from the church. Grid reference 998377.

Map: Ordnance Survey Landranger no. 150, Worcester and the Malverns.

Tea Shop

The Elaine Rippon Shop at Conderton is a most interesting visit but beware that it can prove to be expensive! Husband and wife team, Doug and Elaine Rippon run this silk painting studio. Visitors watch enthralled as this intricate art is demonstrated and made to look so easy. In the retail shop is a beautiful range of silk accessories including ties, waistcoats, earrings, and for do-it-yourself enthusiasts there are even silk painting kits.

Whilst the small coffee shop is really incidental to the business, it is very welcoming. The decor is unusual with some of Elaine's silk pictures on the walls; the bright pottery fish and attractive plants add to the cheery atmosphere. An intentionally limited range of items is available but excellent tea and coffee are served and the cakes are all home-made by local people. Prices are very reasonable.

Open: all the year (except 20th December – 6th January) 10.30am – 5pm but closed Sundays and Mondays except in July, August, and September. If in doubt please telephone first. Tel. 01386 858436.

Description

Having settled the debate concerning the eligibility of Bredon Hill for inclusion in a Cotswold book, we can all enjoy the comparative solitude of this hill and the views in several directions which are a particular feature. The town and vale of Evesham, Tewkesbury, and the main North-western Cotswold scarp with Cleeve Hill, are all prominent.

The iron age hill fort of Conderton Camp lies just over a mile north of Conderton hamlet. Excavations in 1958/9 revealed two phase development of the site, with the later phase (1st. century BC) reducing the overall size of the fort but including a village of circular huts and storage pits. The consequent rises and hollows can still be seen.

Ashton under Hill is one of a string of attractive villages surrounding Bredon Hill, with nice old houses displaying building styles and materials more appropriate to the Vale of Evesham than to the main part of the Cotswolds.

Cottage at Ashton under Hill

The Walk

Walk through the churchyard, where two kissing gates give access to the hillside behind. The initial climb is quite steep, following an arrow to a gate/stile in the top right corner of the field. The odd pause for breath can be used to admire the view behind, Broadway Tower being visible on top of the scarp. Cross a lane to a stile opposite and continue to rise up the grassy hillside, using a sunken trackway higher up and passing

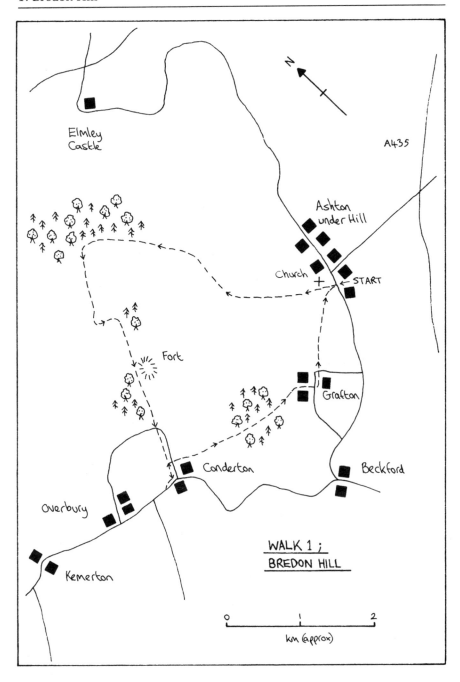

Elmley Castle

A435

Ashton under Hill

Church

START

Fort

Grafton

Conderton

Beckford

Overbury

Kemerton

WALK 1 ;
BREDON HILL

0   1   2
km (approx)

a marker post and stile. The first level top is Beckford Hill (197m), with a well-placed seat.

We are now on the line of the Wychavon Way, going straight across the level area to an arrowed stile 50 yards to the left of the obvious farm gate. The next field is ridged and furrowed and the whole hill does have a feel of ancient occupation. More stiles are all obvious as the route continues to rise, reaching a farm gate with arrow, to the right of the top angle of a field. We are now nearing the summit plateau of Great Hill and the views behind are very extensive, with Nottingham Hill projecting forward from the Cotswold scarp.

Beyond the gate the pasture becomes rougher. Keep most of the hawthorn on your right and follow a sunken track. At the top keep right to follow the edge of a huge ploughed field, apparently more stone than soil in what appears to be natural and traditional sheep grazing country.

The path now keeps close to the top of a scarp, permitting long views over the Vale of Evesham. Unlike so many hill walks, this route has the great advantage of keeping its hard won height for a considerable distance. A wide, wind-swept expanse is crossed to reach a belt of woodland, in which some ornamental conifers have been added to the beech, sycamore and ash.

At the far end of the third huge field, turn left to leave the Wychavon Way at a farm gate, now heading almost due South. The fence on the left soon becomes a wall. Go straight on at a junction, along a broad, grassy swathe, descending slightly. Approximately a quarter of a mile after the junction, turn left at a farm gate to head for a small, isolated, plantation. At an overgrown ruin turn right, downhill, along the bottom of a shallow valley with a wall on the right. As a tree belt is reached on the right, Conderton Camp hill fort is above on the left.

Continue through a gate at the bottom. The broad track here is rather tractor churned and likely to be muddy. It descends directly to Conderton hamlet as a lane and then a surfaced road. At the road junction, the tea shop is a few yards to the right.

Return up the minor road to just above the boundary wall of the Manor and turn right to a "footpath" signpost in 40 yards. The path follows the bottom edge of several fields, a little muddy in places and with some ups and downs. Cross a farm access roadway to head for woodland, with Beckford church tower visible below. The track in the wood is faint, but is not too difficult to follow. There is a bridge over a tiny stream before rising to a stile to exit to open grazing land.

Angle across at about 45 degrees from the boundary of the woodland to a stile below the tallest tree in the hedgerow ahead. Keep the same line across the next field, which is rather rough and hummocky, aiming well above the nearest buildings of Grafton hamlet, making for a farm gate which is just to the right of the house highest up the slope.

Join a roadway and descend through the hamlet. Turn left at the junction and follow this road until it bends sharply to the right. Take the signposted footpath straight on, across a meadow to a bridge with squeezer stiles. Continue along the top edge of a big field, now welcomed by the sight of Ashton under Hill church ahead. A lane leading to the main road is reached, but a notice on a gate insists that "all footpaths are this way". Go through the gate to head for the kissing gate by the church and return to the road.

2. Winchcombe and Cleeve Hill

Length: 10 miles

Summary: Undoubtedly the longest and most strenuous walk in a book of predominantly gentle rambles, this fine circuit will appeal to those who enjoy the freedom of wide open uplands, with the considerable added bonuses of a famous chambered long barrow and the historic little town of Winchcombe. Although the ascent reaches the highest point of the Cotswolds at 1083 feet (329m), the gradients are not too steep and there are no problems underfoot.

Car Parking: In Winchcombe. Vineyard Street, close to public conveniences, is recommended. Grid reference 025282. Alternatively, there is a public car park in Back Lane, off North Street.

Map: Ordnance Survey Landranger no. 163, Cheltenham and Cirencester area.

Tea Shop

The sign outside saying "Ramblers Welcome" attracts the walker to call here at "Lady Jane's Tea Shop". This café seems always to be busy and its popularity is fully justified. The decor is navy and pink – an attractive combination – and there is an inglenook fireplace in the main room.

The menu is wide-ranging with everything available at any time. Lunch choices include Ploughman's with cheese, pate, or ham; fisherman's pie, chilli-con-carne, or perhaps a smoked mackerel salad – there is a big selection! Country lentil crumble sounds an attractive option for vegetarians. Set teas include: "Lady Jane's Cream Tea" – scones, jam, clotted cream, and tea; "Paddington Bear's Tea" – marmalade sandwiches, ice cream, and a cold drink; "Winter Warmer" – pot of tea, toasted crumpets with butter and jam, and home-made cakes. Open every day, 10am – 5pm (closed from mid-January to early March). Tel. 01242 603578.

Description

The history of Winchcombe stretches back into the mists of Saxon times, long before the Norman conquest when, as a walled city, it was head of a district known as Winchcombshire, home of some kings of Mercia. King Offa built a nunnery here in 790 and his successor, Kenulf,

Winchcombe: Victorian almshouses

followed with an abbey in 811. After the murder of Kenulf's son Kenelm (later St Kenelm) the abbey became rich and powerful as a pilgrimage centre. Unfortunately, both nunnery and abbey have disappeared completely, but St Peter's church, close to the site of the abbey, and part built by the Abbot, does provide a positive link with the ecclesiastical past. This is one of the great churches of the Cotswolds with a magnificent clerestory rising above the surrounding town and many treasures inside.

Among the many lovely old houses in this characterful town, the Jacobean House, facing the church, is best known. Of the old inns, the George has a gallery of great antiquity overlooking the yard, claimed by some to date from the times when pilgrims were housed here at the conclusion of their journey.

Modern attractions include a unique Folk and Police Museum in High Street (open from the beginning of April to the end of October), a tiny Railway Museum in Gloucester Street (opening not always predictable), and an abundance of refreshment opportunities. There is also a Tourist Information Office. The terminus of the restored Gloucester Warwickshire Railway, based at Toddington a few miles up the road, and with some steam hauled services, is just outside the town.

Despite all these features, Winchcombe does seem to escape the excessive visitor pressures which sometimes threaten to overwhelm, for example, Broadway and Bourton-on-the-Water.

Belas Knap is regarded as the best false entrance long barrow in the Cotswolds, still extending to 174 feet by 60 feet, and with huge slabs of limestone skilfully placed to form a series of burial chambers which have survived for something like 5000 years. At least 38 skeletons have been found in the various chambers.

Cleeve Common is the largest piece of unenclosed land in the Cotswolds and the only area of true upland character, although its wildness is somewhat tamed by the presence of television masts and a golf course. The top of the scarp is, arguably, the finest viewpoint in the district.

The Walk

Cross the bridge at the bottom of Vineyard Street, heading towards the Studeley Castle gatehouse. Turn right before the gatehouse at a "Cotswold Way" signpost to follow a road for 250 yards. Turn right at a kissing gate with Cotswold Way sign posting and keep to the line indicated by various signs, over stiles and bridges and across fields, the

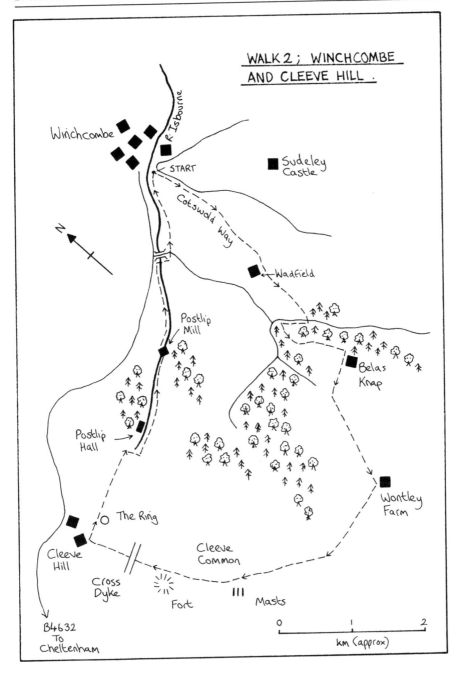

WALK 2 ; WINCHCOMBE
AND CLEEVE HILL .

Winchcombe

R. Isbourne

START

Cotswold Way

Sudeley
Castle

N

Wadfield

Postlip
Mill

Belas
Knap

Postlip
Hall

Wontley
Farm

The Ring

Cleeve
Hill

Cleeve
Common

Cross
Dyke

Fort

III   Masts

B4632
To
Cheltenham

0   1   2

km (approx)

route always well way marked. There is a good view across to Studeley Castle.

The path continues to climb as it hugs the left edge of a rising field to a stile at the top. Winchcombe is well set out behind, with Salter's Hill across the valley. The rather isolated farm of Wadfield is passed as the broad track rises towards Humblebee Cottages, nestling below woodland. Pass the cottages to the right as the path steepens before reaching a minor road.

Turn right, for a long quarter of a mile, still following the Cotswold Way. Turn left at a sign "Belas Knap" to climb steeply through woodland to a kissing gate. Go left to follow the edge of the meadow, soon turning right, uphill. At the top go left through the kissing gate and keep the wall close on your left all the way to the long barrow.

Facing the front of the barrow, turn right, over a stile, to take a path along the edge of a field, and reach a post which gives the distance from Winchcombe as 5km. Bend left along a farm trackway first rising gently across the huge upland expanse and then falling to a farm building (Wontley Farm) in a dip. Turn right here, through a gate, still on the Cotswold Way.

Go uphill again on a good stony track, heading for the television masts. At a gate with a choice of three tracks beyond, take the middle route. You are now rising across Cleeve Common, truly the "roof" of the Cotswolds, real upland common, rich in great clumps of gorse. At the next marker post go straight on although the yellow arrow does point to the right.

Should time or energy be running out, or the weather be ominous, a right turn at any of the various connecting tracks will provide a direct descent to the Postlip area, missing out the top of Cleeve Hill.

For the full circuit continue ahead. As is often the case on a common, there are almost too many inviting tracks, which could cause problems in poor visibility. The most direct route passes about 300 yards to the right of the masts, then heads for a lonely little wind-swept tree on the skyline. However, should you wish to visit the Cleeve Hill iron age promontory hill fort, a deviation to the left not far after the masts will be required.

Bend a little right to continue along the top of the scarp to the now obvious summit, crossing an ancient cross dyke, and enjoying the enormous views. By now you may have realised that you are in the midst of a quite remarkable golf course, which covers much of this end of the common, one green being close to the triangulation point and orientation table at the summit. In view are the Black Mountains, more than 70 miles away, the Clee and Lickey Hills, and the Severn Valley. Closer at hand are Cheltenham, Bredon Hill and much, much, more. By the summit, entwined in the golf course, is the site of an ancient settlement, including the "ring".

Continue by bending right to walk along the top of a valley side, generally above the gorse level, aiming for Winchcombe, ahead. There is a variable but always distinct track. Pass the 8th tee, soon reaching a marker post with arrows. Turn right here to descend very steeply to the valley bottom. In wet weather this section needs considerable care.

At the bottom of the descent bend left at an arrowed post, go over a stile, and cross a paddock between woodland. The route around the boundary wall of Postlip House is well-marked but, unfortunately, nothing more than a glimpse of this building is possible. The clear path continues across an access road and along the edge of the valley bottom woodland before joining a muddy track leading directly into the Postlip Mill complex.

This is clearly a very old mill site, mentioned in the Domesday Book. Originally a corn mill, it converted to paper making early in the 18th century. There are some surviving portions of the old structure **but,** forget all the nostalgia about charming old mill sites. This is now large scale, unattractive, modern industry – West Riding rather than Winchcombe! Pass through quickly, following the arrows which indicate the right of way, heading for the far end of the complex, which does, at least, add variety to the walk!

Exit on a concrete driveway, passing two bungalows, to reach a woodland track. Shortly, ascend the bank on the right to a kissing gate. Go along the edge of the meadow, heading straight for Winchcombe church., then over a stile to the right of a substantial house, angling down towards the fence on the right, reaching the public road at a kissing gate.

Turn right into Corndean Lane and ascend for 100 yards. Turn left at a "footpath" sign and cross the meadow diagonally downhill to a kissing gate leading to the football field. Pass the clubhouse and exit by the main gate. Cross the River Isbourne, turn left then right along the backs to reach the main street by the Jacobean House, just a few yards from Vineyard Street.

3. Winchcombe, Sudeley Castle, and Hailes Abbey

Length: 8 miles

Summary: A good, moderately robust, walk from Winchcombe, passing Sudeley Castle, over Salter's Hill, and down to Hailes Abbey, with an easy return along the Cotswold Way. Steady ascent from Winchcombe to Salter's Hill. The public road known as Salter's Lane makes a pleasant and quiet walking route.

Car Parking: Vineyard Street in Winchcombe, Grid reference 025282, or public car park in Back Lane, off North Street.

Map: Ordnance Survey Landrangers nos. 150, Worcester and the Malverns and 163, Cheltenham and Cirencester area. (As there is a 2km overlap, each of the above maps covers 80% – 90% of the route).

Tea Shop

Just up the lane from Hailes Abbey is the enormous Hayles fruit farm complete with shop selling a good choice of fruit (in September basket after basket of apples, plums, and damsons looked so attractive), vegetables, and preserves including Cotswold honey. The tea shop is housed in a somewhat utilitarian building but the interior is quite satisfactory with a polished wood floor, wooden tables and matching Windsor style chairs. All around the walls are original paintings which are available to purchase. The room is of a good size and it is difficult to imagine it becoming over-crowded. From the large end window are views to Bredon Hill and on a clear day the Malvern Hills can be seen.

Morning coffee with chocolate shortbread or other tempting biscuits is followed by home-made soup, toasted sandwiches, ploughman's (or should it be "fruit picker's"!) lunches and, for tea, toasted tea-cakes, scones, etc. Beverages include tea, coffee, hot chocolate, and cold drinks. Open: All the year except Christmas Day, Boxing Day, and New Year's Day. Tel. 01242 602123.

Description

Winchcombe is described in walk no. 2, Winchcombe and Cleeve Hill.

Sudeley, "England's most romantic castle" is a major stately home, surrounded by beautiful gardens and park land, set at the foot of the slopes of the nearby hills. The present castle was built by Ralph Boteler in the 15th century, although there was an earlier castle on the same site. There were strong royal connections in Tudor and Elizabethan times and, after the death of Henry VIII, his surviving Queen, Katherine Parr, brought the Court to Sudeley on her re-marriage. She is buried in the adjacent St Mary's Chapel.

During the civil war Sudeley was for some time a Royalist headquarters and was badly damaged by Cromwell's army, the chapel being desecrated. The ruins of the Elizabethan banqueting hall still bear witness to the turbulence of this period of the castle's history. Otherwise restored, the castle has many art treasures and modern attractions such as an exhibition centre. Part of the interior and all external features are open to the public daily from 1st. April to 31st. October; the gardens, plant centre, shop and restaurant are also open in March; the shop and plant centre are open for three weeks in December.

St Kenelm's Well could hardly present more of a contrast. A tiny, chapel-like building accessible only on foot, with a carved stone over the door, marks the place at which those bearing the body of Kenelm back to Winchcombe Abbey, after his murder at Clent, rested. Kenelm was the young son of King Kenulf, founder of the Abbey.

Unlike Winchcombe, the ruins of the Cistercian abbey at Hailes still survive. Allegedly founded by Richard, Earl of Cornwall, a son of King John who, after leading the crusade to the Holy Land in 1240, became head of the Holy Roman Empire for fourteen years, this abbey became a place of pilgrimage of international repute. Richard is said to be buried at Hailes, although his heart was taken to Oxford.

Inevitably destroyed by Henry VIII, the ruin was totally neglected for centuries, becoming badly overgrown. Now cleared, and managed by English Heritage on behalf of the National Trust, the site gives a fair impression of the past glory of this great abbey, which had a church of cathedral size. A collection of fragments of the sculptured stone has been assembled and is displayed on site. (open daily from 1st. April to the end of October; Wednesday to Sunday from November to March).

Across the road the little church of Hailes is even older than the Abbey, although it was rebuilt at about the time of the construction of its great neighbour. The passing of the centuries has enriched its basically Norman origins with additions such as the panels of glass from the Abbey in the 14th century east window, the medieval paintings on the chancel walls, and the fine oak chancel screen. The timbered bellcot adds a touch of quaintness to the generally plain exterior.

Hailes church

The Walk

Set off down Vineyard Street, at the south end of Winchcombe. There are signs on the main street for both the Cotswold Way and the Windrush Way. On reaching the Sudeley Castle gatehouse, take the castle access drive, apparently part of the Warden's Way. Cross a substantial bridge by a small lake.

By a cattle grid, fork right at a farm gate to follow a well-worn track, with the Sudeley Castle adventure playground to the left. Go straight ahead to a kissing gate. Although the way keeps close to the boundary fence, there are only tantalising glimpses of the castle itself.

As the fence turns sharp left, continue across the huge meadow, to a stile in the far right corner. There are helpful arrows on some of the cages protecting young trees, and a prominent dead tree is a good first indicator of the line. Go over the stile, then another, following yellow arrows, then up the left hand edge of a field, bending right along the top edge. Turn left at a plank bridge and stile to rise to the farm access roadway close by a pair of cottages which have been very much in view for most of the way.

Turn left to walk to the public road, then left, downhill, for 60 yards.

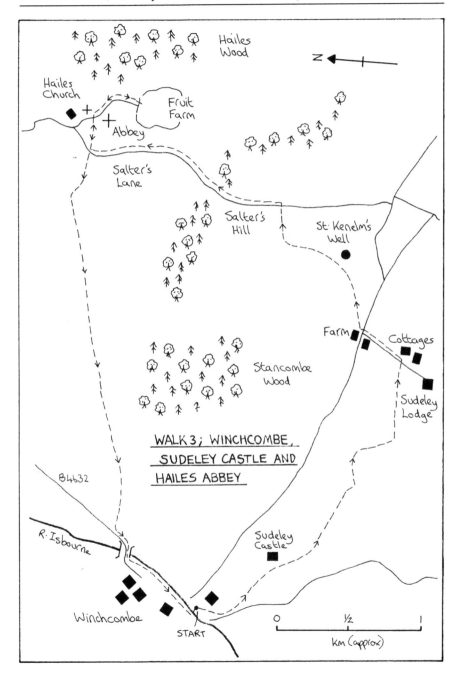

Hailes Wood

Z ←—⊢

Hailes Church

Fruit Farm

Abbey

Salter's Lane

Salter's Hill

St. Kenelm's Well

Farm

Cottages

Sudeley Lodge

Stancombe Wood

WALK 3; WINCHCOMBE,
SUDELEY CASTLE AND
HAILES ABBEY

B4632

R. Isbourne

Sudeley Castle

Winchcombe

START

0   ½   1

km (approx)

Just above Sudeley Hill Farm is a footpath sign on the right. Follow the route indicated, rising diagonally across a large field, keeping left of huge old horse chestnut trees, to a gate/stile ahead. Continue on the same line, joining a rough surfaced farm track at a gate with yellow arrow, bearing left.

To the right is the locked building at St Kenelm's Well. Continue to a gate with yellow arrow, and then diagonally across a large rising field, making for a gate in the top left corner (depending on crops, it might be necessary to detour around the edge of this field). Follow the edge of the next field to reach the public road, crossing part of the broad top of Salter's Hill.

Turn left, along the road known as Salter's Way, soon heading downhill past Little Farmcote, with wonderful open views across the Vale towards Evesham. In rather more than one mile, at the bottom of the hill, look out for a footpath on the right, part of the Cotswold Way, heading straight for Hailes church. Take this to join the minor road by the church. Turn right to the Abbey ruins, and continue along the road to the Hayles fruit farm and tea rooms, a further 300 yards.

After refreshment, return to the church and retrace the Cotswold Way route across the field opposite. At the lane, turn right, then left in 100 yards at yet another Cotswold Way signpost. A good, but possibly muddy, track rises gently. Look carefully for a post on the left with a yellow arrow pointing to a right turn on a grassy path along the edge of a field.

The route is generally well-marked, over stiles and through kissing gates. To the left is the Cotswold scarp with roughish sheep grazing country, whilst to the right are the richer lands of the Vale of Evesham, with Bredon Hill prominent.

Winchcombe comes into view over the brow of the hill, and there is a steady descent to a wooden bridge, followed by stiles and an unsurfaced, tree-lined, lane. This leads into the built-up area and, as Puck Pit Lane, joins the main road. Turn left to walk into Winchcombe, crossing the River Isbourne on the way. The main thoroughfare comprises a fascinating jumble of property, with many low buildings having the characteristic little Cotswold dormer windows. There are also several timber framed structures.

By the junction with North Street is the Tourist Information Centre; continue along the main street, passing a car parking area, before Vineyard Street is reached.

4. Buckland and Broadway

Length: 4 miles

Summary: A fairly straightforward walk linking two very different villages, with easy ascent and no real difficulty underfoot.

Car Parking: In Buckland only rather obtrusive roadside parking is possible. Accordingly, use of the cleared portion of land by the roadside at the junction of the Buckland village road and the main road is recommended. Grid reference 074364.

Map: Ordnance Survey Landranger no. 150, Worcester and the Malverns.

Tea Shop

Popular with people from all over the world, Broadway is always busy. There is considerable choice of tea shops in this town and we sampled three of them.

1. "The Master's Pantry" can be found by turning right at the church (just after leaving the field path and joining the road) and following the sign-post for car park and toilets. It is at the top of a small modern precinct of shops. There is a comprehensive menu including excellent coffee served in individual cafetières, Danish pastries, cream teas, and "very up-market" Grand Marnier cheesecake. Savouries include raised pies, salads, sandwiches, etc. Inside is pleasing pine furniture and intriguing and tempting views of the delicatessen counter, whilst outside the tables are in a sheltered and sunny situation.

2. "Roberto's Coffee House" – from the path, walk towards the town and turn right when approaching the main road – Roberto's fronts onto The Green at the bottom of the main street. The menu is varied and ranges from hot pasties – popular on cooler days – to ice-cream. The most mouth-watering of all are perhaps the enormous saucer shaped meringues filled with fresh cream. For sale at the counter are bear-shaped jars of Cotswold honey. Outside are tables overlooking the Green, and sufficiently away from the never-ending flow of traffic passing by on the main road through Broadway.

3. "Small Talk Tea Shoppe" – is to be found on the left mid-way along High Street. Cakes, pastries and bread are sold at the counter, whilst behind is quite a large café. The all-day menu offers toasted sandwiches, open sandwiches, filled jacket potatoes, cream teas, plus the usual range of beverages.

The Old Rectory, Buckland

Description

Broadway, in Worcestershire, is one of the great Cotswold honeypots, its broad street, lined with chestnut trees and rising towards the Cotswold scarp, being thronged with visitors for much of the year. Fortunately, the weight of tourism has done little to spoil the excellence of the old Cotswold buildings of this most English of villages, beloved of William Morris, Elgar and Vaughan Williams. These buildings date from many periods of history and include the Lygon Arms, in part 16th century, Abbot Grange of the 14th century, and Tudor House of 1660.

The original parish church of St Eadburgh is situated about one mile to the south, on the Snowshill road, but St Michael's was built much closer to the village in Victorian times. Shops of all kinds abound, with no lack of hostelries (it is claimed that at one time there were no less than 33 in the village!) and other refreshment places.

In complete contrast, Buckland is an entirely peaceful backwater on a cul de sac road, but with good buildings including the mainly 15th century church and the oldest inhabited rectory in Britain.

The Walk

Walk for 400 yards along the road into Buckland, which continues as the village street, with no lack of charming houses. On the left, immediately after a footpath sign, is the Old Rectory. Stay with the road as it passes the church and bends left, uphill, to pass a newish holiday complex and former mill dams.

At the top of the rise, just after a prominent agricultural building, turn left to join the Cotswold Way at a stile. After a second stile, follow an arrow pointing along the edge of a field. Follow the arrows from stile to stile and enter woodland at a gate, turning right. In 100 yards or so turn right again, going downhill to leave the woodland at a little gate.

Broadway village is now well seen across a large meadow, although one housing estate does strike a jarring note. Continue with the woodland close on the left, then turn right to descend to West End via a made up footpath at the bottom. Cross the lane and head for the church, crossing a well-constructed wooden bridge provided by the Cotswold Voluntary Warden Service.

Bear left by the church to reach the village centre and choose your tea shop as advised above.

To return to Buckland, retrace your steps as far as West End Lane. Across the lane, take the footpath forking right signposted "Buckland". After two stiles, cross a large rising meadow, aiming for a stile roughly

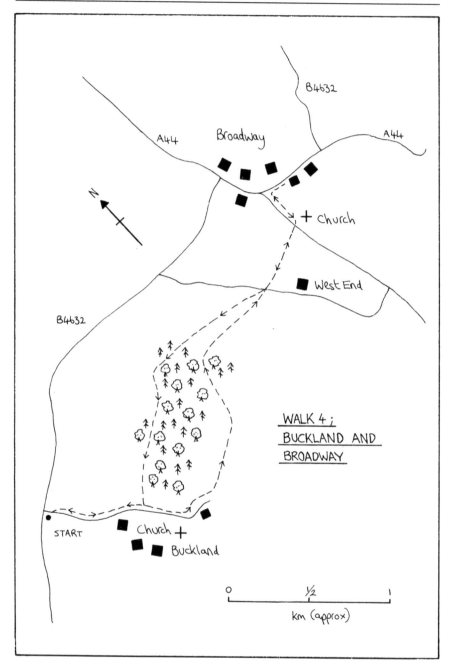

in the middle of the top boundary of the field. Go straight ahead in the ensuing woodland. As the track forks, keep straight on, on the level, along the bottom edge of the woodland.

At the next apparent fork, a route either to left or right of the fence may be chosen. The open country to the right now permits long views across the Vale of Evesham and to Bredon Hill. A further woodland section may well be muddy; an autumn compensation could well be the prolific blackberries along the way.

At a gate, emerge on to open hillside to continue along a good green track facing Bredon Hill. Beyond a stile are three possible routes, all arrow marked. Take the middle way, keeping fairly level across the hillside, with the vast expanse of glass at Buckland Nurseries below to the right. A steep little downhill leads to a gate/stile and a grassy track between the gardens leading to Buckland village street. Immediately on the left is the rear elevation of the Old Rectory.

Turn right to return to the car park.

5. *Snowshill*

Length: 5 miles

Summary: This fine circuit includes the village of Snowshill, with its celebrated Manor House, a length of the Cotswold Way along the northern part of the escarpment, and the site of Shenberrow iron age hill fort. The ascent of the scarp is from the rear and at comparatively gentle gradients. Apart from a little mud, there are no problems underfoot.

Car Parking Public car park adjacent to the entrance to the car park serving Snowshill Manor. Grid reference 096340.

Map: Ordnance Survey Landranger sheet no. 150, Worcester and Malverns.

Tea Shop

First the bad news! – this rather super restaurant is accessed through the ticket office and therefore is available only to visitors to Snowshill Manor and/or gardens and paying admission charges, or to National

Tea room at Snowshill Manor

Trust members who are, of course, admitted to the property without payment. The good news is that Piper's Grove restaurant (new in 1995) serves a variety of food for lunches and teas. Included on the menu are the National Trust Special Ploughman's Lunch with Gloucester Single and Cotswold cheeses, Snowshill pate with toast, and numerous tempting savoury dishes. Scones with jam and clotted cream and a good selection of cakes are served, with a choice of tea or coffee; the list of cold drinks includes elderflower lemonade. The café is spacious and inviting. Outside is a large terrace with inspiring views across to Shenberrow Hill. Incidentally, any profit from this enterprise contributes directly to the conservation work of the National Trust.

Open April and October daily (except Tuesdays and Good Friday): noon – 4.30pm, May to end September (except Tuesdays): noon – 5.30pm. Also restaurant and shop open weekends all November and until mid-December but advisable to check by telephone. Closed completely January, February, and March. Will open for some of Easter weekend if this falls in March. Tel. 01386 858685.

Description

Quite remote for access despite its proximity to Broadway, Snowshill village falls prettily down the side of its own valley, with a tiny green by the church and the inn. Surprisingly small, the Manor, owned by the National Trust, is of paramount interest. Dating in part from around 1500, this traditional local stone building is complemented by a terraced garden replete with old fashioned roses and shrubs. At least equally remarkable is the collection of curios amassed by Charles Paget Wade, filling the Manor House. Wade himself lived very modestly in an outbuilding at the rear, without modern facilities. His living quarters can still be seen by visitors to the Manor.

Normal National Trust seasonal opening arrangements apply, the property being open during the afternoon (not Tuesdays) from April until the end of October.

Shenberrow Hill is a part of the north west facing Cotswold scarp, with long views to Evesham and Bredon Hill. The iron age hill fort, whilst not one of the finest of the 17 situated along the scarp, does have much of the twin defensive mounding visible; various artefacts were unearthed from the site during some excavation work carried out in the 1930s.

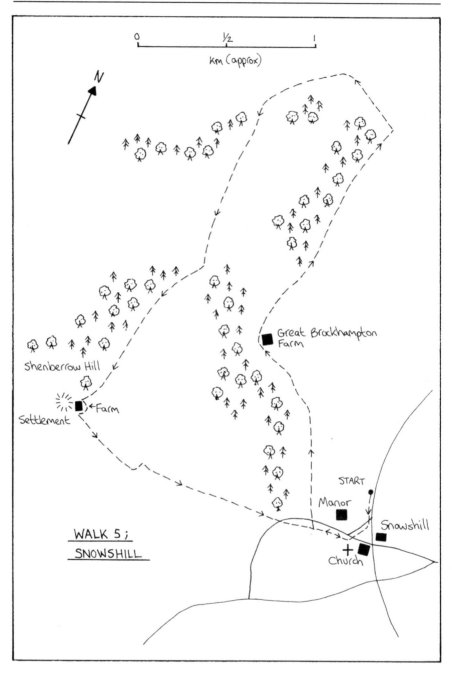

WALK 5;
SNOWSHILL

The Walk

Turn right from the car park to walk along the road, and descend through the village, passing the tiny green between the Snowshill Arms and the church. There are some very attractive buildings along the way.

Just before the road begins to climb, turn right at a "public footpath" signpost to descend initially. At a gate with a "private property – keep out" notice, the path goes to the left, keeping close to the fence on the right, over well-cropped grass. After a stile, the path rises, becoming a little muddy, to a gate. A wide pasture follows, with the track just about visible as it aims to the left of Great Brockhampton Farm, ahead. Go over the stile, cross the farm access road and take the track opposite, which angles to the right, behind the farm buildings.

Follow the farm road which for some distance splendidly traverses the long hillside, with extensive views over Snowshill and its vale. For about one mile no route finding is necessary. As the track bends left around the far end of the hill, to a gate, there is a wonderful "surprise" view over the Vale of Evesham and as far beyond as clarity of the atmosphere will permit.

In a further 30 yards bear left up short grass towards a marker post with arrow, continuing to another post before descending to join the Cotswold Way by a fence. Turn left to follow the Way. Below is Buckland village as the Way rises gently towards the highest part of the scarp. Ignore any deviations and stay with the Way, enjoying the long views of high ground (Cleeve Hill) to the south west, in addition to the fine views to the north.

At a junction of tracks, keep to the Cotswold Way as it turns sharp right over a cattle grid, continuing to rise along the edge of woodland to reach Shenberrow hill fort. The defensive strength of the position in countering any threat from the Severn valley or the Vale of Evesham is very apparent.

Turn left into a marked public bridleway, traverse the buildings of Shenberrow Hill Farm, then turn left on a good but possibly muddy track. The summit of the hill, at 304 metres, is close on the left but, in the absence of a marker, is not easy to distinguish in this rolling hill country. Turn left at a "T" junction and, in 40 yards, turn right at a post with faded arrow.

The track angles to the left diagonally across a field to a gate in a wall, then continues the same line, downhill, directly towards Snowshill. A farm gate giving access to a surfaced farm road is reached. Turn right to carry on towards the village, soon joining the public road and turning left to return to the car park and the Snowshill Manor tea shop.

6. Chipping Camden and Dover's Hill

Length: 2¼ miles (4 miles with extension)

Summary: From Chipping Camden up to Dover Hill and back is a short, straightforward, walk, mainly on footpaths, with a steady climb and an easy return along part of the Cotswold Way.

Car Parking: There is designated roadside parking in Back Ends, parallel with the main street, reached by turning off the main street at the Volunteer Inn. Grid reference 149392.

Map: Ordnance Survey Landranger no. 151, Stratford-upon-Avon and surrounding area.

Tea Shop

Chipping Campden is a near perfect small town and there are a number of tea shops. We visited and enjoyed "Forbes". This spotlessly clean, rather sophisticated restaurant has a very welcoming notice at the door saying "between 9.30am and 10pm it is always a pleasure to serve you". However, discretion is called for and it would not be appropriate to arrive here in really muddy boots and dripping cagoule.

The decor is really good, with old family photographs, copper canopy sheltering a welcoming blazing fire, albeit an imitation one. The servery is laid out with irresistible pastries and other temptations.

The menu is extensive ranging from English breakfast, morning coffee, shortbread, bacon and egg baps, through to afternoon teas (between 3pm and 6.30pm there is a minimum charge per person, but no obligation to have a set tea). Bistro-style food is served too; the blackboard menu when we were there included noisettes of lamb, Cornish skate with black butter, and many other imaginative dishes including desserts. Beverages include a good choice of teas, coffees, etc. and for something quite different why not try elderflower presse!

Open every day, 9.30am to 10pm (closed during the Christmas period). Tel. 01386 840330.

Chipping Camden market building

Description

Chipping (Saxon "ceping" – market) Camden was one of the great medieval wool towns of the Cotswolds and the buildings, particularly the parish church of St James, show abundant evidence of the consequent prosperity. One of the best known of the many wealthy wool merchants was William Grevel, mentioned by Chaucer in the "Canterbury Tales". Grevel was a great benefactor of the church and his 14th century house in High Street remains almost unchanged. The town motto is "History in Stone" – golden, glowing, Cotswold limestone all around and showing particularly well in the Jacobean market hall and the Woolstaplers' Hall of 1340, which is now a delightful museum, open every day from the beginning of April to the end of October. Close to the church is a particularly fine row of almshouses.

Perhaps best of all is St James's church itself, an imposing edifice of remarkably consistent design and with a wealth of interest inside, including brass and marble effigies of many great wool merchants. Possibly unique are a cope and altar hangings of the 14th and 15th centuries respectively.

As part of the Cotswold escarpment, Dover's Hill is a fine amphitheatre, noted as a viewpoint, The hill was probably the site of Whitsuntide games from very early times, but the famous "Cotswold Olympick Games" were started here in 1612 by Robert Dover. The emphasis was on hard physical contests such as shin kicking and combat with long sticks, in addition to foot racing and hare coursing. In the early 19th century as many as 30,000 people attended the games, but by mid-century criminal and unruly elements prevailed and there was a series of riots. Not surprisingly there were many complaints and the games ceased in 1853.

The land was acquired by the National Trust in 1928 and the games, in a modified form, were revived in 1951, taking place at the traditional Whitsuntide.

Down the North-west slope of the escarpment, the Lynches woodland includes a terraced bank which was cultivated in medieval times when there was demand for extra plough land. At least some of the strip lynchets in this area are believed to have been used as vineyards in the Romano-British period.

The Walk

From the car parking area walk back (west) to pass the bottom of Hoo Lane and leave the road as it bends left towards the town centre. In 30 yards follow a footpath sign on the right. The path weaves ingeniously upwards between houses and gardens.

Cross a residential road, turning left for 30 yards, then right at a sign, eventually reaching open country after a development of modern stone houses.

Rise across a long abandoned orchard, the way being indicated by a stile and yellow arrows. On reaching a very large cultivated field, follow the hedge boundary on the right for 40 yards and then strike straight across on the same line., heading for a just visible sign on a post at the far side.

Turn left at the road (Kingscombe Lane) and, in a short distance, turn right at a signposted footpath which leads to the summit of Dover's Hill, with its "topograph". Unless the walk is to be extended (see below), turn right along the crest of the scarp, soon reaching Bold Gap at the far end.

Turn right to follow the Cotswold Way. At a post with arrows, turn right (yellow arrow) over a stile and along the edge of a field to return to the road. Turn left and, in less than 100 yards, turn right to continue along the Cotswold Way, being careful to take the made up section of path at a fork. A farm track is joined, descending very obviously direct

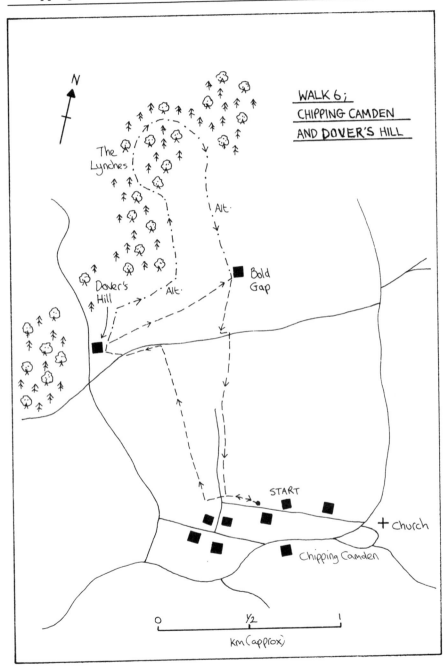

The Lynches

Alt.

Bold Gap

Dover's Hill

Alt.

Alt.

WALK 6;
CHIPPING CAMDEN
AND DOVER'S HILL

START

Church

Chipping Camden

0   ½   1

km (approx)

to the town, via Hoo Lane. The main street (High Street) is reached at the Volunteer Inn, with the tea shop and main part of the town to the left.

Extension

This is a route for lovers of good, varied, woodland, organised and signposted by the National Trust. There is a considerable fall and rise from the start at the "topograph".

Go steeply downhill, heading for the minor road on the left, to a post which points the way to Lynches Wood. Follow the indicated line towards a gap in the hawthorns by a little pond, soon reaching a second post, which is to the right of the best line. Bend left at the next post, downhill all the way, keeping close to the left hand field boundary.

Enter the wood at a stile numbered "1". There is a numbered marker at each significant point on this route through the extensive wood. A longish flight of steps requires care during or after wet weather. After bearing left at the foot of the steps, the track curves right for some distance to traverse this very diverse woodland, left in an apparently natural, little managed, condition by the Trust. At sign no. 8 the wood is left at a gate and stile and the track rises along the left edge of the huge sheep pasture.

At the top corner are several tracks. Take the gate/stile straight ahead. An N.T. post points to Bold Gap. At a gate with blue arrow continue over well-cropped grass to a post with three arrows at the North-east end of the Dover's Hill scarp, where the basic route is re-joined.

7. Hidcote Manor and Mickleton

Length: 3¼ miles

Summary: From Mickleton village, a walk up the hillside through varied countryside to the internationally famous Hidcote Manor Gardens, returning by a different but straightforward route. The ascent is steady, without any particular difficulty. Bearing in mind the alternative refreshment possibilities set out under "tea shop" below, there is no reason why Hidcote should not be used as the start/finish of the walk should this be preferred.

Car Parking: Find a roadside space in Mickleton. Grid reference 161438.

Map: Ordnance Survey Landranger no. 151, Stratford-upon-Avon and surrounding area.

Tea Shop

The choice of tea venue for this walk will need to depend upon the day of the week and the month of the year!

At Hidcote Gardens there are two facilities – the main restaurant is accessed only when visiting the gardens, or by presentation of a National Trust membership card. Here is a selection of food ranging from the "National Trust Special Ploughman's Lunch or "Hidcote Pate Platter" to coffee, tea, cakes, and scones. The opening hours are 11am – 5pm from Easter/1st April to the end of October, daily (except Tuesdays and Fridays).

The second option at Hidcote Gardens is at the Plant Sales Centre which is fully accessible to the public irrespective of visiting the gardens or of membership of the National Trust. Tea, coffee, ices, cakes, etc. are served in a very pleasant sheltered courtyard beside the thatched barn but please note that there is no indoor seating here. This amenity is open from April to the end of September from 10.30am – 5.30pm daily. The telephone number for Hidcote Manor Gardens is 01386 438333.

The alternative to Hidcote is quite different in character but very interesting. Open weekends only but all the year round is the tea room at Myrtle House in Mickleton. This enterprise is ran by Gilly Hogg and her husband, Richard. The menu has tempting old fashioned varieties of cake such as Victoria sponge, chocolate cake, and lemon drizzle slice. Also available are toasted tea-cakes, buttered scones, iced buns, tea, coffee, lemonade, and glasses of milk. There is a foot-note on the menu "please ask if there is something you would like that is not listed" – a nice touch! Be assured that Gilly will do her best to please.

The Hoggs are a young family with wide-ranging interests and a good knowledge of the area – Richard is a qualified tourist guide. They offer bed and breakfast with an optional evening meal every day throughout the year but the tea room is open only on Saturdays and Sundays from 10.30am – 6pm. Tel. 01386 438003.

Description

The National Trust owned Hidcote Manor Gardens, just three miles north-east of Chipping Camden, comprises a most alluring series of small gardens, each with its own distinctive character. The usual National Trust opening season of April to the end of October applies to the gardens and to the licensed restaurant. There are plant sales until the end of September.

Mickleton drinking trough

On the whole, Mickleton would win no awards as the prettiest village in the Cotswolds, but it is by no means without interest. It is very much a two-part settlement, with a nondescript modern extension to a much nicer old part, which has some timber framed and dormered houses. The use of brick tends to confirm the position as a Cotswold fringe village. The church has substantial Norman features and an elegant spire more than 600 years old.

The route of the walk passes by another garden, Kiftsgate Court, particularly noted for its collection of roses. It is open to the public on Wednesday, Thursday and Sunday afternoons from April to September, on Saturday afternoons in June and July, and on Bank Holiday Monday afternoons.

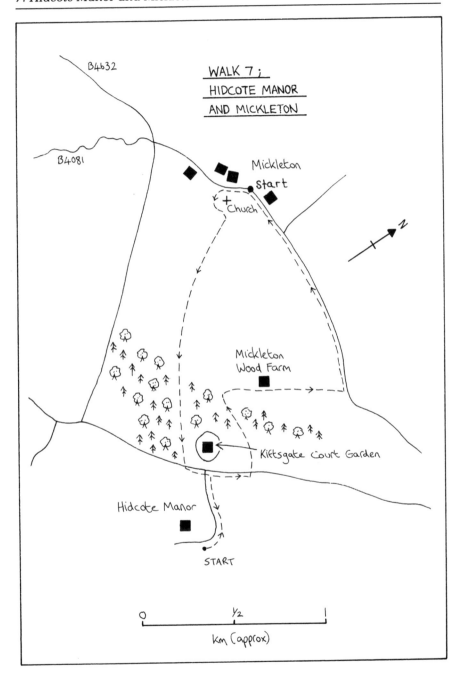

The Walk

Walk to the parish church, just off the main street. Behind the church no less than three footpaths set off up the hill towards Hidcote. Probably the best is the designated bridleway, Pass between the church and the burial ground, through a gate, then turn right across a small meadow towards a small gate with blue arrow.

A well-used path keeps to the right hand boundary of a big field, close to a tiny stream, bending left at the top to a gate. A broad, grassy, track continues to rise across a large meadow, just below woodland, to a farm gate in the top left corner, with a muddy area. Continue uphill along the grassy bottom of a shallow valley, heading for a wall and ornamental gate pillars at the top. Just when it seems that there is no way out and scaling the wall is a serious consideration, a wide gate is found on the right.

Exit, cross the road, and take the minor, signposted, road leading directly to Hidcote Manor Gardens.

Return by the same route as far as the road, by the entrance to Kiftsgate Court Gardens. Turn right, along the road, for about 300 yards, then turn left at a farm type trackway with yellow arrow. There are good long views across the Vale of Evesham and, closer at hand, the rooftops of Mickleton at the foot of the scarp. The track dips to descend through woodland, varied but with beech and oak prominent.

As the track forks at the bottom of the wood, go right to cross a sloping meadow to Mickleton Wood Farm. Pass through the farm and along the access drive to the public road. Turn left and follow the road through the newer and much less attractive part of the village to return to your vehicle.

8. *Bourton-on-the-Hill and Blockley*

Length: 5 miles

Summary: A partially circular walk, up and over the broad ridge which separates the well-known villages of Bourton-on-the-Hill and Blockley, and along the edge of the Batsford estate. There is a steady climb of 300 – 350 feet on each side of the ridge and the route includes some distance on a minor road with a short section alongside the main A44 through Bourton.

Car Parking: On the minor roadway behind the church in Bourton. Grid reference 176324.

Map: Ordnance Survey Landranger no. 151, Stratford-upon-Avon and surrounding area.

Tea Shop

Lady Northwick's Tea Shop in Post Office Square is small but enjoys a big reputation; the visitors' book proves that people come here from all over the world so Patrick Barton is justly proud its international fame.

There is a large table laden with home-made cakes of unusual varieties including orange and almond cake, carrot cake and Auntie Sue's Cotswold apple cake!

Light lunches are available including sandwiches, salads, vegetarian quiche. "The big Cornish pasty" served with onion gravy would be delicious on a cold day. A choice of coffee and tea is offered. In hot weather one could be tempted by one of the new range of iced teas; these are real teas with added fruit flavours including peach and raspberry.

Opening hours are generally 11am – 5pm (closed Mondays) and closed in winter except for weekends. It would be advisable to telephone first. Tel. 01386 701202.

An alternative venue for sustenance would be The Crown Inn, Blockley.

Description

Although one of the larger Cotswold villages, situated within 4 miles of

Street scene, Blockley

Chipping Camden, Blockley is just sufficiently off the beaten track to avoid becoming a "tourist" village. With the odd little shop, several inns and, of course, the tea shop, it still has a "lived in" air, very much a village for local people.

That doesn't mean that it is without attraction for visitors. The stream flowing strongly through the deep valley encouraged the development of water powered mills for a variety of purposes. After the general decline in the woollen industry, came the trade in silk ribbon and, only 100 years ago, there were six mills involved, employing several hundred people. All the mills are now converted to other use, primarily residential, but the buildings still add to the variety of the architecture, with the deep, warmly golden cast of the local stone, one of the most attractive in the Cotswolds.

The impressive church shows a mixture of styles, from the Norman onwards, as the building has been modified many times over the centuries. South of the village, the valley was landscaped by John Rushout, the second Lord Northwick, of the nearby Northwick Manor, and was given the misleading name of "Dovedale" in the 19th century.

The smaller village of Bourton-on-the-Hill climbs steeply up the side of the ridge, facing Moreton-in-Marsh in the wide valley bottom below.

Although cottages, church and inn make an attractive combination, the overall effect is unfortunately diminished by the village street being the main A44 road between Moreton-in-Marsh and Broadway.

The little church of St Lawrence has work from the 11th century onwards, including a 14th century font which was found buried in the churchyard and restored in 1900. Also in the church is a Winchester bushel made of bell metal, dating from the time of Elizabeth I, when the Winchester measures were of such accuracy that they set the standard for the whole of the Kingdom, particularly in disputes concerning the weight of corn tithes. A little lead figure of St Lawrence is in a niche above the porch.

At the foot of the hill, Bourton House is a fine 16th century manor, with a celebrated old barn, whilst a short distance to the south Sezincote is a sizeable park land estate, with an early 19th century house built in an Indian (Moorish according to some) style. It is said to have influenced the Prince Regent in his design for the Brighton Pavilion.

Sleepy Hollow Farm Park, close to Blockley, has a collection of rare breeds of domestic animals, pet centre, picnic areas and refreshments. (open daily from mid-March – check date – to October).

The Batsford estate and arboretum is described in walk no. 9, Moreton-in-Marsh and Batsford.

The Walk

Start by walking down the A44 towards Moreton-in-Marsh, passing a terrace of houses "The Retreat for the Aged", erected in 1831, then Bourton House. Beyond the built-up area, turn left at the driveway signposted to Batsford Arboretum and Falconry Centre. A long roadway, bordered by young trees, heads straight for the Centre, only the lodge being visible at the far end.

Opposite the lodge turn left at a gate to follow a track across a field towards a stile at the far side, part of the "Heart of England Way". Note the pronounced "ridge and furrow" configuration of this meadow. A few yards of narrow path lead to an unmade roadway. Turn left to continue steadily uphill below fine, mature trees, largely oaks and beeches.

At a long left bend, turn right towards the estate wall then, almost immediately, left before a gate to follow the wall, uphill, eventually reaching a minor road at a gate. Go straight across to two farm gates side by side, with a yellow arrow. Take the right hand gate and keep to the

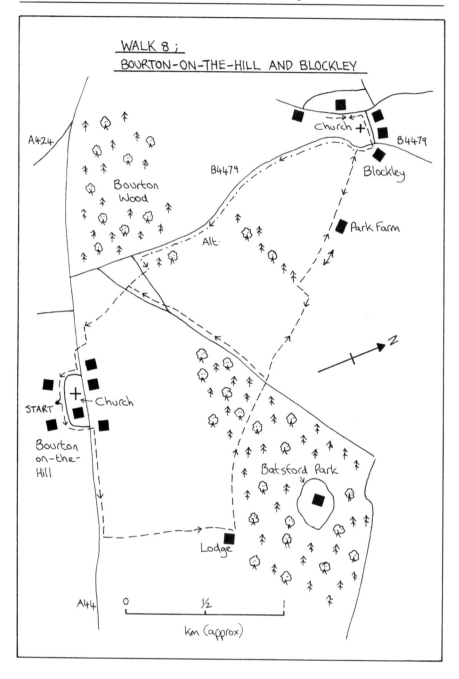

edge of the field, passing plenty of brambles before Blockley comes into view ahead.

A "T" junction is reached at an old lane. Turn left for a short distance, then right at a gate/stile, to descend over farmland straight towards Blockley. The track is just visible on the ground, keeping a few yards from the field boundary on the right. Park farm below is passed by a stile to its left and yellow arrows point the way to join the public road at the bottom.

Turn right into Blockley, then left and left again to the tea shop, church and main part of the village.

For the return to Bourton there are options, including the obvious retracing of the outward route. For a partial circuit, the following is recommended.

Retrace the outward route as far as the minor road. Turn right to walk towards the junction with the more important road B4479, forking left in a quarter of a mile. In 200 yards or so after the fork, turn left at a stile and take a farm type track heading for the left hand end of a belt of woodland. Keep straight on at a fork, gently downhill.

Turn left at a stile towards Manor Farm, then right just before the farm yard entrance to reach the main A44 road. Turn left to descend to Bourton.

9. Moreton-in-Marsh and Batsford

Length: 4½ miles

Summary: An easy walk over almost level ground, based on Moreton-in-Marsh, using field paths and a quiet lane to visit Batsford Park and its famed arboretum. No hills or quagmires, although the odd field might have a ploughed-over footpath.

Car Parking: Except on market day (Tuesday), there is plenty of street parking in Moreton. Typical grid reference 205325.

Map: Ordnance Survey Landranger no. 151, Stratford-upon-Avon and surrounding area.

Tea Shop

"The Apple Store" is tucked away behind the garden centre and by the entrance to the Batsford Arboreteum. The outside seating is in a sheltered, pleasant and restful environment.

The menu includes "The gardener's light lunch" with chunky home-made soup and granary bread. Also available are salads, broccoli and tomato quiche. For tea, scones, buttered apricot bread, cakes, good coffee made in individual filters, and of course pots of tea.

Open April to end of October, every day: 11am – 4.30pm. Tel. 01386 700409. When closed, or as an alternative, there is a good choice of tea shops in Moreton-in-Marsh. We can recommend Townend Cottage (almost opposite Budgens Supermarket) – very busy, especially on market day, but pleasantly helpful staff. Tel. 01608 650846.

Description

The well-known little market town of Moreton-in-Marsh, in the northern part of the Cotswolds, has the Roman Foss Way as its wide main street, lined with generally handsome buildings, largely of the 18th and 19th centuries. Over this period the town grew significantly, due to the thriving coaching trade, followed by the arrival of the railway in the mid-19th century. Moreton is one of the few of the smaller Cotswold settlements still to have a rail passenger service. There was also a linen

The market, Moreton-in-Marsh

weaving industry which grew following the decline of the traditional woollen industry. The Tuesday street market is justly renowned and the town generally has a lively bustle, with plenty of shops and refreshment opportunities.

The "marsh" part of the name is liable to misunderstanding. Although the land around Moreton is pretty flat and is not infrequently wet underfoot, it is not a swamp, the "marsh" being a corruption of "march", an ancient name for a boundary. Until 1928, four counties came together at four shires stone, about two miles east of the town. Following reorganisation, there are now only three, Worcestershire having retreated for ten miles or so to the north-west, but Moreton is still a boundary town.

The oldest building is the 16th century curfew tower on the corner of Oxford Street, still housing the curfew bell dated 1633, which was rung daily until the mid-19th century. Dominant on High Street is the Redesdale Hall, also known as the Market Hall.

The magnificent Batsford Arboretum was designed and planted by Lord Redesdale in the 1880s. Having spent some time in Japan, he introduced a distinctly Japanese element into the Arboretum including a large bronze Buddha at the top of the hill. In more recent years the second Lord Dulverton has greatly increased the number and diversity of the trees, particularly magnolias and maples. A charge is made for entry to the Arboretum, which is open from the beginning of March to early November, as is the adjacent Falconry Centre. The garden centre is open all the year. The large house, which has an "estate" village at the rear, is not open to the public.

The Walk

Walk to the northern end of the main street in Moreton. Just before the bridge over the railway (by the supermarket), turn left at a footpath sign, pass a children's play area, turn sharp right, under a huge oak tree, to steps up to the public road.

Go across the road to a small gate almost opposite and cross a large meadow, at first keeping roughly parallel with the railway line, which is behind the line of trees to the right. Bend left to a small gate in the far corner. After a second gate go straight ahead with the hedge boundary on the right.

At Dorn, turn left along the surfaced minor road, heading towards Batsford, the house soon being visible among the trees ahead. At a junction keep straight ahead, the road now being lined with mature

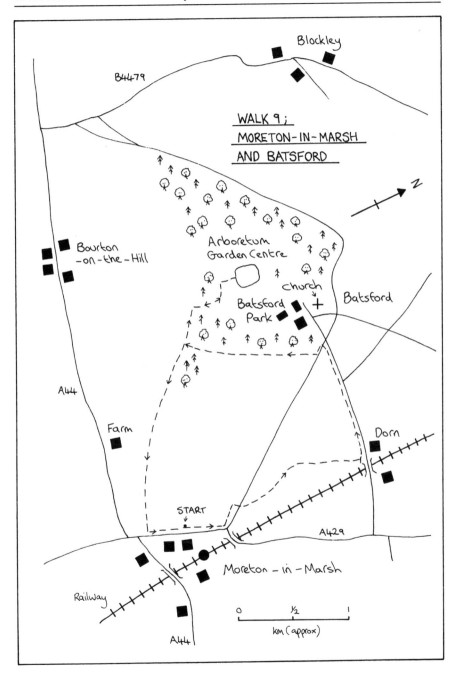

WALK 9;
MORETON-IN-MARSH
AND BATSFORD

Blockley

B4479

↗ Z

Bourton
-on-the-Hill

Arboretum
Garden Centre

church

Batsford

Batsford
Park

A44

Farm

Dorn

START

A429

Moreton - in - Marsh

Railway

A44

0   ½   1
km (approx)

trees, predominantly oak, with some ash, making a very pleasant walking route.

At a cross roads the road ahead leads into the Batsford estate village with its 19th century church. For the circuit turn left at the cross roads towards Moreton. In 60 yards turn right at a farm gate/stile with yellow arrow. A well-trodden and way marked path proceeds in a more or less straight line along the edge of Batsford Park, over several stiles. Look out for the deer in the park land to the right and for a closer view of the house. Pheasants are also plentiful. Towards the end of this path a field has been ploughed too close to the boundary and mud could be a nuisance in wet weather.

After a final gate a post with four footpath signs is reached. Turn right here to the Batsford lodge, then follow the access roadway to the car parking area, garden centre, tea shop and other attractions, including the arboretum.

After refreshment, return to the four footpath post and go straight on towards Moreton, through an arrowed kissing gate, following a barely visible track about 20 yards from the boundary on the left. Keep to roughly the same line, through more gates, now closer to the boundary, over a stone bridge. The path now goes straight across a field which will probably be cultivated, to yet another kissing gate, heading for Moreton, visible ahead.

At the side of the paddock-like dog walking area of a large caravan site, turn left at a kissing gate, then right, to enter the town alongside allotments. Go straight ahead to the main street. There are public conveniences just to the right.

10. Long Compton and The Rollright Stones

Length: 5 miles

Summary: The highlight of this walk is undoubtedly the celebrated cluster of fine Neolithic features known collectively as the Rollright Stones, which are close together by the minor road which runs along the top of a broad ridge at the north-east extremity of the Cotswolds. The walk is generally easy, although the north side of the ridge must be climbed right at the outset. This is neither steep nor prolonged and is the only ascent in the whole circuit. There is more than the usual amount of road walking but, with the exception of the short length of the main A3400, the roads are truly minor; in particular the road descending to Long Compton is hardly more than a farm lane.

Car Parking: There is a useful small lay-by at the junction of the main A3400 and a minor road at the south end of Long Compton. Grid reference, 290320.

Map: Ordnance Survey Landranger no. 151, Stratford-upon-Avon and surrounding area.

Tea Shop

Wyatt's Farm Tea Room was a surprise find. We had hoped to find a tea shop near to the Rollright Stones and this was a super discovery! The tea room is linked to a very good and justifiably popular farm-shop which sells quality vegetables, cheese, an incredible range of unusual preserves and many other goodies – well worth a browse for Christmas presents.

The café itself is spacious, spotless, and super! It is counter-service with friendly young staff in attendance, offering a good variety of food, available all day. The menu includes hot soup, quiche, jacket potatoes etc. and on Sundays people flock here for the highly regarded roast lunches. Being tea time, we sampled cherry scones and chocolate cake; both were judged to be mouthwatering.

Open: all the year (except the Christmas period) 10am – 5pm winter; 10am – 6pm summer. Tel. 01608 684835.

Description

The Rollright Stones have had a considerable mystical fame since medieval times, when peasants would chip pieces off in the belief that possession would keep away the devil and there is, inevitably, a legend concerning a king and a witch. The three separate features are:

The circle of almost 60 stones known as the Kings Men, which stands on privately owned land and in respect of which a small charge (proceeds to animal charities) is made. Many still appear to believe in the supposed mystical properties of these stones and it is not uncommon to see visitors walking in a trance-like state holding out their arms as if directed by some external force.

The isolated King's Stone stands on the other side of the road; some believe it to be the sole residue of a long barrow burial chamber, the remainder of which has long disappeared as a result of ploughing.

The Whispering Knights are situated 400 yards or so to the east of the main circle. They are comprised of a group of four upright stones, with a fifth stone which was originally a capstone. This group was the portal at the end of a long barrow, no other traces of which now exist.

Although not yet dated with any precision, these stone age monuments are likely to be about 4000 years old.

Lych gate, Long Compton

The most interesting feature in Long Compton is the very unusual thatched lych gate, with a room over the gate. Unfortunately the A3400 road is normally busy and does rather detract from the enjoyment of this village by walkers. In addition to the excellent tea shop, Wyatt's Fruit Farm, at Hill Barn, has a large shop with fresh produce and a very wide range of country products, both usual and not so usual.

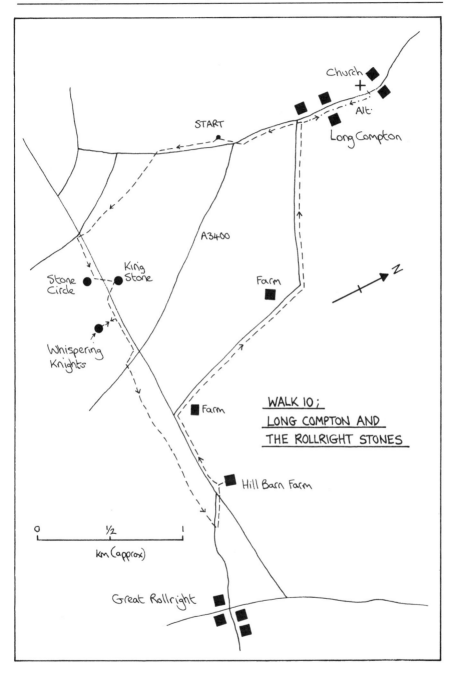

The Walk

Proceed up the minor road for half a mile. As the road bends to the right, go through a gap on the left to angle uphill along the edge of a field, with a hedge on your left. The gradient eases and, as the hedge terminates, keep to the same line for another 200 yards or so, aiming for a gap with a house behind. Join the road and turn left.

The stone circle is soon reached, sitting behind the hedge on the right. After visiting the circle, continue along the road for a few yards and go over a stile on the left to look at the King's Stone, standing isolated in a field. You will also notice a board advertising the Wyatt's Farm shop and tea rooms; don't get too excited yet – there is still a fair way to go before refreshment! A few hundred yards further along the road, at a farm gate, a track on the right leads to the third stone age feature, the so-called "Whispering Knights". The views from this point are far ranging, and the hedgerows are rich in bramble.

Return again to the road and walk to the junction with the main road A3400. Turn right along the roadside for about 150 yards, looking carefully for a not very obvious flight of stone steps on the far side of the road. Ascend the steps to a sign "footpath Gt. Rollright 1" and follow the well-established track across the fields of this wide spaced upland countryside. At a double farm gate, turn left, then left again at the nearby road junction. In rather more than 100 yards turn right to Wyatt's farm shop and tea room.

Eventually tearing oneself away from this fascinating place, return to the road and turn right. In half a mile, turn right again to take a very minor unsignposted roadway, descending past another fruit farm and returning all the way to Long Compton.

A left turn at the main road returns straight to the car parking lay-by. However, Long Compton is not without interest, and a diversion as far as the church at the far end, either on foot, preferably using the back roads, or by car, is recommended.

11. Stow-on-the-Wold, Broadwell and Maugersbury

Length: 7 miles

Summary: An interesting circuit combining the fine Cotswold town of Stow-on-the-Wold with several varied villages. Not all the tracks are well-used, but there are no difficulties underfoot and the two uphill sections are neither steep nor unduly prolonged. The B4450, along which there is a roadside section of the walk, is not a busy road.

Car Parking: Find a suitable roadside space in Upper Oddington village, Grid reference 225257, or Lower Oddington village, half a mile or so along the minor road to the east.

Map: Ordnance Survey, Landranger no. 163, Cheltenham and Cirencester area.

Tea Shop

There are so many tea shops in Stow-on-the Wold that it is not easy to choose just one but who can resist the name "Shepherd on the Hill"? Entering this tiny café (which seats only twenty-four) is like entering someone's front room. Classical music is played at a suitably low volume to permit conversation whilst avoiding a feeling of unease if sitting alone or wishing to be silent. Horse racing memorabilia adorns one wall ; on another is a dresser laden with preserves available to purchase. The uniform china is the lovely Royal Worcester "Evesham" pattern which is appropriate as the Worcestershire border and the Vale of Evesham are not too far from here.

The full menu is served all day including the hot dishes which range from lasagne with salad to sirloin steak with chipped potatoes. An alluring choice of cakes are displayed and cream teas are always available. Drinks include tea, coffee, fruit juices, but why not have a change and try the speciality of the house "shepherd's special" – hot chocolate with brandy and whipped cream – delicious!

Open all the year (closed every Wednesday) 10am – 5.30pm and sometimes later! Tel. 01451 831526.

Description

The market town of Stow-on-the-Wold "where the wind blows cold" is set high, at nearly 800 feet, on true wold country to the north-east of the district. Perhaps owing something of its fame to its charming name, Stow is also an important communication centre, with roads radiating in all directions. There was also once a minor railway which fringed to the town, to the south.

When the wool trade was flourishing, Stow, like other Cotswold towns, became wealthy, with a market charter as early as 1107, and two annual fairs filling its fine market place, where old cross and stocks still stand close by. The centrally situated parish church of St Edward has Norman origins and was used as a prison for defeated Royalist troops after the battle of Donnington in 1646. There are many excellent town houses, including the handsome St Edward's, and, as Stow is a busy centre, shops, inns, and other refreshment houses are plentiful. In comparatively recent years the town has become noted for its trade in antiques.

Broadwell, Maugersbury and Lower and Upper Oddington are four villages of varied character, all worth a visit by those who appreciate groupings of beautiful buildings in local Cotswold stone set in rolling

Upper Oddington

countryside. In particular, Maugersbury seems to be much quieter and more remote than would be expected from its distance of only half a mile or so from the bustle of Stow.

The Walk

Walk along the road through Upper Oddington, passing the allegedly 16th century Horse and Groom Inn. At the end of the village, at a tiny green, the former footpath has recently been diverted. Continue along the road for more than 100 yards and turn right at a stile, with footpath sign, along a made up path.

At the end of this new section, turn left to keep close to the field boundary, heading just to the left of a mound created by a covered reservoir, to a kissing gate. Head for the large rugby clubhouse, the correct line being behind the building, followed by a left turn at a farm gate, along a bridleway between fields, to reach the public road (B4450).

Turn right along the road and go as far as the junction with the A436, with the tower of Stow church appearing on the horizon ahead. Turn left here to follow the surfaced lane winding attractively to Maugersbury. Bear left to pass through the village and, at the bottom of the road, before a cul de sac sign, turn right between gate pillars.

The road soon loses its surface, passing Maugersbury Manor and many holiday cottages as it rises to Stow, reached by the side of a car park with public conveniences, near the Bell Inn. Turn left up Sheep Street. The tea shop is on the left.

From the tea shop cross the road and go straight ahead to the Market Place, passing the Royalist Hotel which is claimed to be the oldest in England, quoting a rather unlikely date of 947 AD, entry in the Guinness Book of Records, leper holes, witches' marks and other strange curiosities.

Leave Stow Market Place to the north, heading for the main road to, inter alia, Moreton-in-Marsh. Turn right before the main junction and go downhill. As the road turns sharp right, turn left by Stow surgery to follow a cul de sac roadway. At once we are out of the built up area with long views over lovely wolds countryside. Stow Well is passed – a spring with a large stone trough.

The way becomes a stony track, then a straight but narrow path between walls. Join a minor road and turn right, downhill, to reach Broadwell village with its spacious and well-kept green. The route here lies to the right, but a diversion to the left is needed to visit the church, the inn, and the tiny ford. To leave Broadwell, take the road towards

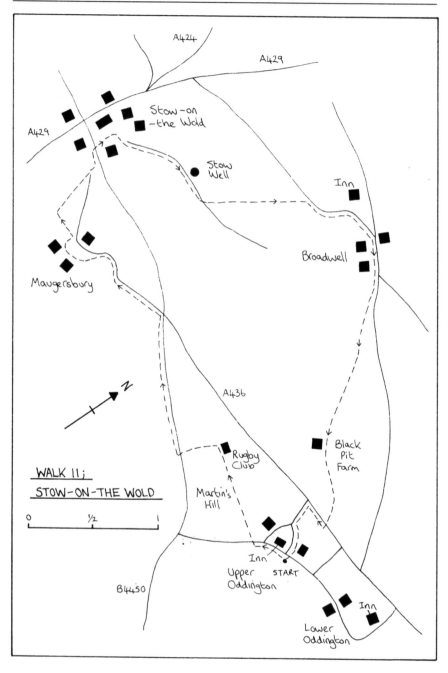

WALK 11;
STOW-ON-THE WOLD

Evenlode and Oddington. After passing a sizeable farm, and before the last house in the village, turn right at a farm gate with footpath sign.

The path goes very obviously straight ahead through flattish farming country, entirely peaceful and contrasting sharply with the hustle and bustle which is inherent to so much of the Cotswolds. Keep the hedge boundary close to your left all the way to a shallow valley, where a tributary stream of the River Evenlode is crossed on a bridge. Go up to a gate/stile with yellow arrow and follow the indicated direction, half right diagonally across a huge field. There is a faint track on the ground, aiming for a small marker post just to the left of a double telegraph pole.

Bear left at the far boundary, along the edge of the next field, to reach the farm at Black Pit. Go through the farm and continue along the access drive to the main road. Turn right, then left, to return to Upper Oddington. Turn left, then right, to return to Lower Oddington.

12. Bledington and Nether Westcote

Length: 6½ miles

Summary: A varied walk, mainly in the broad valley of the River Evenlode, visiting lesser known villages and the extensive Herbert's Heath woodland on the eastern fringe of the area. The ascent of the valley side is quite gentle and some mud is the only likely hazard. The road between Idbury and Nether Westcote is very quiet indeed.

Car Parking: Find a discreet roadside space in Bledington village. Typical grid reference 245227.

Map: Ordnance Survey Landranger no. 163, Cheltenham and Cirencester area.

Tea Shop

"Cotswold View" is one of those pleasant surprises! We had never heard of Nether Westcote – a very small rural hamlet – and noticed the tea shop signs posted on the main Stow to Burford road. This "off the beaten track" tea room is part of a guest house owned by Tony and Hazel Gibson. Teas are served in the dining room and in the conservatory. Tony is the waiter and service is pleasant and efficient. Good choice of the usual tea-time specialities including sandwiches, cakes, freshly baked scones with clotted cream and jam, and a selection of teas including Earl Grey and herbal varieties.

Every lunch time, soup is available and is served with a cheese scone. On Sundays the traditional roast lunch is a popular option but it would hardly be possible to do justice to afternoon tea afterwards!

Bed and breakfast is available here; evening meals are served but must be prior booked.

Open seven days each week, 10am – 5pm, from Easter/1st April to end of October. Tel. 01993 830699.

Description

Despite its proximity to Stow-on-the-Wold, not everyone in Gloucestershire could readily direct you to Bledington, definitely one of the lesser known villages of the far east of the county. It is, nevertheless, an attractive old village, sitting close by the River Evenlode, with a May pole crowned by a weather-vane in the form of a fox on its green. The largely Norman church is well worth a visit.

Nether Westcote and Idbury, both in Oxfordshire, are two of a string of small, east facing, villages sited just below the crest of the Evenlode valley side. The clerestoried church at Idbury has some good internal features, including a fine old font and 15th century carved bench ends.

Nether Westcote

The Walk

From Bledington walk along the main road towards Kingham station. As the road turns sharp left in about a third of a mile, go straight on along a minor road leading to Foscot and Idbury. In 150 yards turn left at a sign "Oxfordshire Way". Go over a cattle grid to a farm gate with blue arrow and turn right, along the edge of a big field. The extent of use is evident from the hoof marks.

The level track follows the bottom of the valley of the River Evenlode, so flat and wide that to those from the Lake District or the Yorkshire Dales, it is hardly a valley at all! No route finding is necessary nor are

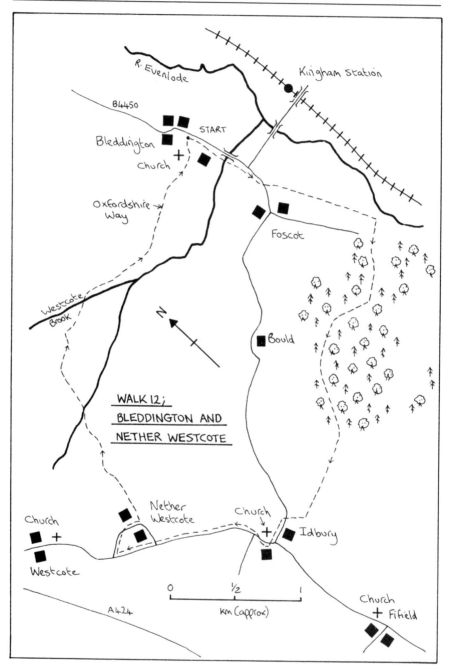

R. Evenlode

Kingham Station

B4450

START

Bleddington

Church

Oxfordshire Way

Westcote Brook

N

Foscot

Bould

WALK 12;
BLEDDINGTON AND
NETHER WESTCOTE

Nether Westcote

Church

Church

Idbury

Westcote

A424

0   ½   1

km (approx)

Church
Fifield

there any stiles or gates for some distance, but the path does have its muddy sections.

Don't miss a sharp left turn (blue arrow) at the edge of a plantation, soon turning right to resume the original direction, along the side of a drainage ditch. Turn right at a blue arrow by the side of a bridge over the ditch, to head for woodland. At a post with several blue arrows keep straight on to join a rough surfaced lane, with buildings to left and right.

At the top of the lane go through a farm type gate, along the edge of a field to another gate at the top, and take a muddy track through the woodland, rising gently. At a junction of tracks by a post with blue arrow, follow the main track, now on the edge of the woodland. Ignore any paths to left or right and continue through the attractively varied woodland, with plenty of beech and oak, bramble in the undergrowth, and evidence of coppicing.

Within the wood there is an abundance of paths, some being rights of way whilst others give access to different parts of the nature reserve. Many paths wind about considerably and it is not unlikely that the route here suggested will be lost at some stage. However, the overall objective is to head uphill to the top edge of the wood.

At a "Berkshire, Buckinghamshire and Oxfordshire Naturalists Trust – Nature Reserve" sign turn right for rather less than 400 yards and then left at a junction. Oaks and silver birch are now prolific. As the path forks, keep right. There are now many conifers on the right, then an old mobile hut of the type formerly used by shepherds in some parts of the country.

At a "T" junction turn left, now close to the edge of the wood, reaching a board with information about the Site of Special Scientific Interest, which is, in part, a remnant of the ancient Wychwood Forest. From here, keep to a path as close inside the edge of the woodland as possible, but avoid leaving the wood at any of the openings into the adjoining fields. The objective is to reach the furthest upper extremity of the wood at a point where there is a sharp angle. The last section of this path is somewhat overgrown.

On reaching the point at the south-west corner, leave the wood, turning right to follow a track pointed out by a bridleway arrow and well-trodden across a cultivated field. Idbury church, with tower, is now the obvious destination and the way is no longer in doubt. After the first field the route is unploughed, the gentle rise to Idbury reminding us that the Evenlode does, after all, have a valley.

As Idbury is reached, turn right, through a farm gate, towards the church, then through another gate to reach the public road. Turn left, passing the parish church of St Nicholas and a distinctive toll house on the left as the road curves right.

At the road junction go straight on for Nether Westcote, along the minor road which keeps to the crest above the valley, with correspondingly wide views. At Nether Westcote, pass the first road junction, turn right at the second, pass the Methodist church and, in 50 yards, find the Cotswold View Guest House and Tea Room.

From the tea shop turn left, downhill, though the lower part of the hamlet, passing the New Inn. As the road bends back to the right, turn left, downhill, into a stony lane, signposted as a bridleway. The lane provides very easy walking, but is rather churned by the passage of horses. Some way down, a stile with yellow arrow on the left offers an alternative track along the edge of the adjacent field, definitely preferable during or after wet weather.

On reaching the end of the lane, or the alternative footpath, continue along the field edge for 150 yards or so, to a large open meadow. Follow the path worn beside the left hand boundary, to a wooden post with blue arrow "Oxfordshire Way – bridleway". Turn sharp right here. An obvious field edge path now leads to a gate and a plank bridge, turning right to another small gate, and then an artificially constructed animal watering place, with bridge over the Westcote Brook.

Don't cross, but carry straight on, the Oxfordshire Way now being a footpath with yellow arrows but still apparently horse churned. The Way goes straight on at further junctions, then angles across two cultivated fields, Bledington village coming into view at this point. After another plank bridge and stile, ascend the left hand edge of a meadow with defunct wind pump. After more arrowed stiles, cross the burial ground behind the church and return to your parking place.

13. Burford and Widford

Length: 6 miles

Summary: The very popular little town of Burford is the base for a circular walk which starts along the placid River Windrush, visits Widford church, and returns across farming country. There is very little ascent and, apart from the usual mud, no problems underfoot. Roadside walking is kept to a minimum and is not unpleasant.

Car Parking: Excellent free car park in Burford, by the river at the lower end of the town. Grid reference 254126.

Map: Ordnance Survey Landranger no. 163, Cheltenham and Cirencester area.

Tea Shop

Burford and Huffkins Tea Shop are synonymous with everything English. This busy venue is a perfect example of the type of eating place unique to this country and of which we British should be justly proud.

To start with the early part of the day – Huffkins offer a "Cotswold Breakfast" which includes a pair of kippers and grilled tomatoes. One choice for lunch would be their "Fisherman's Lunch" – smoked mackerel with garnish and wholemeal bread or, alternatively, the "Farmer's Lunch" – cold roast beef and pickles – might tempt the appetite. For tea – "Huffkins Cream Tea" or the "Burford Tea", which includes sandwiches.

The above are just examples from the very wide menu, from which most items are available throughout the day. Beverages include hot chocolate, hot milk with honey and nutmeg, milk shakes, varieties of coffee – capuccino, expresso, Viennese or iced. The range of teas is similarly extensive, ranging from Huffkin's own tea-room blend to vintage Darjeeling.

There is also a shop counter with a selection of teas, coffees, delectable preserves, delicious cakes and Belgian chocolates.

Open daily 9.30am – 5.30pm but closed on Sundays, Christmas Day and New Year's Day. Tel. 01993 822126.

Description

Burford seems to compete with the equally popular town of Broadway for the title of "Gateway to the Cotswolds" Another feature common to the two towns is a fine wide rising main street, in Burford's case rising directly from the River Windrush. In Burford, this street has a stunning array of the houses of the woollen merchants and others who brought wealth and importance to the town from the 15th century onwards. The predominant stone in Burford is one of the finest of all Cotswold limestones, quarried at nearby Taynton for many centuries. The same stone was used by Wren in constructing the dome of St Paul's cathedral.

Even among this wonderful array of buildings, the parish church is still outstanding. Most of what we see, including the superb south porch, is the result of extensive refurbishment in the 15th century, but the church still has identifiable work of the 13th century, when the previous substantial renovation was carried out. In the churchyard are the "wool sack" gravestones of some of Burford's rich merchants.

The origins of the town go back to Saxon times, when the ford across the River Windrush was a part of a route between Wessex and Mercia, a battle between the two kingdoms being fought nearby. In later times, the house named the Priory was the home of William Lenthall, famous as the Speaker who defied King Charles I when he entered the House of Commons to arrest five members. Another episode in Burford's history occurred a few years later, in 1649, when some mutineers from Cromwell's army were captured and imprisoned in the church for three days, three of them then being taken into the churchyard and shot, as an example to the others, who had to watch the execution.

One 16th century house, The Tolsey (Court House) now houses a museum (open during the afternoon, from Easter to October), and there is a Tourist Information Office. The Cotswold Wild Life Park is just over two miles to the south of the town.

There could hardly be a greater contrast than that between Burford and the simple little church of St Oswald at the "lost" village of Widford. It is presumed that the Black Death was responsible for the disappearance of this community, which had 13 households in the 14th century, and just three in the 16th century, now all gone without trace. The Saxon church was rebuilt around 1100, over the floor of a Roman villa, a section of the pavement being discovered and exposed, together with 14th century murals, in 1904, forty years after the church had fallen into disuse.

Unfortunately, the pavement has been re-covered to prevent vandalism, but the primitive interior, with box pews, is still worth seeing.

The Walk

Leave the car park over the access bridge crossing the River Windrush and go up to the minor road which heads east from Burford. Turn left by the Great House, close to the Royal Oak Inn, and pass the old bell foundry and some charming cottages. After leaving the built-up area, the tree lined road remains entirely pleasant.

In a little more than half a mile turn left at a stile with "Widford 1" signpost. The ensuing delightful riverside path is easy to follow, with arrowed stiles pointing the way. As the path becomes squeezed between river and road, join the road and then turn left at a road junction by Widford Mill Farm. There is a sign "circular walk, Widford".

Cross the river, then turn right at a cattle grid to follow a broad track towards St Oswald's. Divert for a few yards to visit the quaint little church. Back on course, bend left to a gate with yellow arrow and signpost and then rise along the bottom of a shallow valley with woodland on either side, that to the right being rather dull coniferous, but with a much more attractive mixture on the left.

On reaching the surfaced lane at the top, turn right for 300 yards or so, then left into a broad trackway descending to a gate with both blue and yellow arrows. Take the blue, firstly along an inviting terrace rising ahead, then by the edge of woodland, to a gate/stile and an unsurfaced lane going downhill to a surfaced road.

Turn left, uphill, passing Paynes Farm and a terrace of cottages, as the lane leads to Widney Copse. Go straight ahead at a junction. The ruler-straight way through the wood makes the far exit look like the portal of a tunnel.

On leaving the woodland, turn left immediately, to follow the line indicated by a yellow arrow (and wheel marks on the ground) across a huge cultivated field. Eventually the far side is reached at a gap in a wall. Go through and keep to the left hand boundary of the next field, turning right at the corner to continue along the boundary.

In another 150 yards, turn left at a gap in the hedge and follow the yellow arrow to cross another large cultivated field, again with wheel marks along the line. At the far side, a little post with yellow arrow confirms that the right line has been taken. Turn right, along the field boundary, to reach the main A361 road via a narrow path through the nettles.

Turn left into Fulbrook, passing the Masons Arms, the Church (away to the right), and then the Carpenters Arms. The church and the rooftops of Burford are obvious below as the road descends to a roundabout.

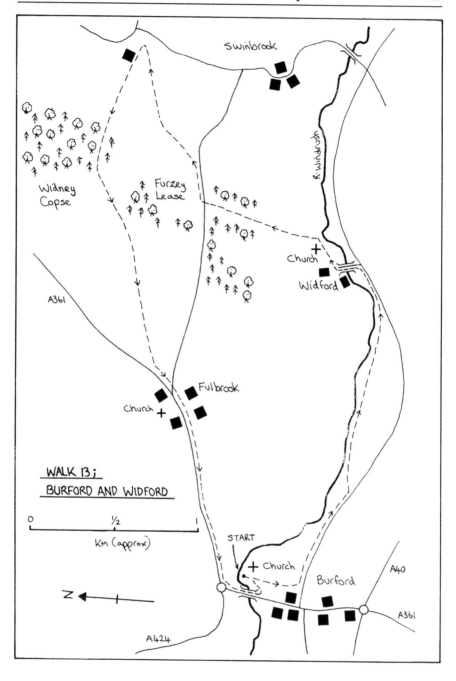

Swinbrook

R. Windrush

Widney
Copse

Furzey
Lease

Church
Widford

A361

Fulbrook

Church

WALK 13;
BURFORD AND WIDFORD

0   ½   1

Km (approx)

Z

START

Church

Burford

A40

A361

A424

Turn left and cross the traffic-controlled road bridge into the main street. The tea shop is higher up, on the right. Perhaps after refreshment, do leave a little time for the church and the adjacent almshouses, close to the car park.

For a shorter walk, turn left at the lane above St Oswald's Church, Widford, and walk along almost one mile of pleasant very minor road to Fulbrook.

14. Broadwell, Langford and Filkins

Length: 4¼ miles

Summary: Truly one of the easiest walks in the book, totally without ascent, visiting villages which others neglect, together with the Cotswold Woollen Weavers Centre.

Car Parking: In Broadwell. A small roadside lay-by outside the village hall, by a telephone kiosk. Grid reference 252040.

Map: Ordnance Survey Landranger no. 163, Cheltenham and Cirencester area.

Tea Shop

A visit to Cotswold Woollen Weavers could prove expensive, as the shop offers a variety of attractive materials woven on the premises,

ready-made clothes, and gifts. However, it is quite possible to avoid temptation in the shop, only to be confronted with different temptations in the coffee shop! Situated at the centre of the complex, the café is adjacent to a sheltered, well-groomed grassy area where one can partake of refreshments when the weather permits. The menu is short but there is sufficient choice of food and drink, including delicious cakes.

Open 10am – 5pm (later at busy periods)

Looms at Cotswold Woollen Weavers

every day throughout the year except from Christmas Day until 1st January. Tel. 01367 860491.

The tea shop at Cotswold Woollen Weavers

Description

You may be forgiven for not being totally familiar with Broadwell, Langford and Filkins or, indeed, with Broughton Poggs. All are unpretentious and very genuine rural settlements on flat farming land just to the east of the A361 main road between Burford and Lechlade, a few miles north of the River Thames.

Apart from the Cotswold Woollen Weavers premises at Filkins, the most notable feature in each case is the church, three fine and varied examples being included in the circuit.

Langford is the most substantial of the villages and has a church of particular interest with some unique features. A Norman tower constructed on a Saxon base, fine Norman doorways and 14th century carvings of the crucifixion on the outside of the porch, are just some of the attractions of this lovely building.

Next on the route is Broughton Poggs, not much more than an old Manor House, or Hall, with large farm and church in close attendance.

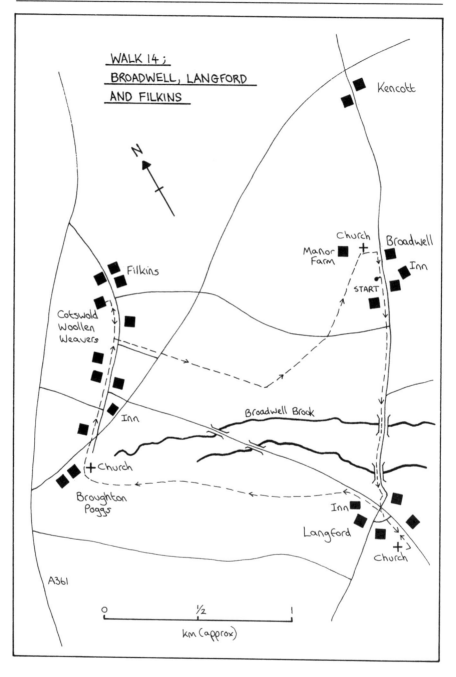

WALK 14 ;
BROADWELL, LANGFORD
AND FILKINS

Here the church is simpler, but with many Norman features, including the low tower with its saddleback roof, barely clearing the nave.

Filkins has the tiny rural life museum established by the late Sir Stafford Cripps to house the collection largely amassed by the late George Swinford (unfortunately, open to the public on only five days per annum, although it may be opened at other times by appointment tel. 01367 860334). In contrast, the Cotswold Woollen Weavers Centre is open daily throughout the year. Tastefully renovated 18th century buildings house traditional woollen weaving and ancillary equipment which, combined with craft workshops such as stonemasonry, leather working and rush seating, and, not least, the tea shop, make a deservedly popular visitor centre. Entry is without charge and the shop sells woollen goods made on the premises.

Finally, back to Broadwell, and yet another fine church, again predominantly Norman, with a beautiful doorway and a great tower arch. There is also a 13th century font and, nearby, the remains of an ancient cross.

The Walk

Start by heading south down the road towards Langford. This is a very quiet road, suitable for a leisurely ramble such as this, with time to admire the roadside properties along the way. Broadwell Brook is crossed as Langford is approached. The bulk of the village, with some lovely dormer-windowed houses and the church, is to the left and a small deviation from the circuit is highly recommended. The church is found on the right, towards the far end of the village street.

Return to the road junction and go straight ahead to follow the "Filkins and Burford" sign, passing a small chapel. As the road bends right, go through a farm gate on the left, with arrow and signpost. Keep close to the edges of several fields, through farm gates and over stiles. When the hedge on the left ends, strike boldly across a cultivated field, along a helpful wheel track, to a plank bridge and stile about 25 yards to the right of the corner of the hedge opposite. Continue roughly the same line across a meadow, to a gate, with Broughton Poggs now in view.

Bend a little left across farm mud to a stile to the left of the church. Cross a paddock to another stile. Divert right through a small gate to visit the church, which is very much enclosed by Broughton Hall and Manor Farm.

Back on course, from the churchyard iron gate go straight ahead to a wooden gate/door in the wall opposite, not signposted, and then bend right along a driveway in the grounds of the Hall, passing a pond and tennis court before reaching the public road.

Turn right, then bear left at the road junction, to pass the Five Alls Inn and Filkins church. Next along the road is the Lamb Inn, followed by the Swinford museum and the Cotswold Woollen Weavers Centre.

From the Centre, turn right, back along the road, to Hazells Lane, first on the left. Turn left along the lane among delightful cottages, with good examples of the flag on edge boundary walls which are common in Filkins but very unusual in the Cotswolds generally, being more reminiscent of Hawkshead, in the Lake District. Cross a more important road to a wide gap in the hedge, on the opposite side, and follow a just visible path along the left hand edge of a cultivated field to a gate/stile in the left corner.

There is a yellow arrow here and we are informed that we are joining the D'Arcy Dalton Way. Follow the line indicated by the arrow, staying quite close to the hedge on the left, through a farm gate, and keep the same line across the next meadow, heading for Broadwell church, with its graceful spire.

Go over a stile 30 yards to the right of a farm gate, cross a minor road to another stile and take the left hand of the two paths indicated by yellow arrows, to another stile under a large hawthorn. Turn right along a broad trackway, passing an impressive house with ornamental pond. Either continue to the road or divert left to a small gate giving access to the churchyard.

In either case, turn right along the road for a short distance to return to the parking place. Note the two massive stone pillars on the right which are all that remains of a hall burned down many years ago, and the stepped base, presumably of an old cross, now surmounted by a rather incongruous modern column.

15. Windrush and The Barringtons

Length: 6 miles

Summary: A circular walk with very little ascent, predominantly through farming countryside, never far from the River Windrush, visiting three well known Cotswold villages and their focal point, the Fox Inn.

Car Parking: In Windrush village. In front of the church is as good a place as any. Grid reference 193130.

Map: Ordnance Survey Landranger no. 163, Cheltenham and Cirencester area.

Tea Shop

Because of the lack of a tea shop, we hesitated to include this walk. However, it is a very attractive ramble, and passes a welcoming hostelry, so we think this can be the one exemption in the book.

There is a very comprehensive menu at The Fox, ranging from hot meals to sandwiches and the speciality of the day listed on the blackboard. The whole range of drinks is available and good quality coffee is served. Regrettably afternoon tea is not usually available here, but of course, if preferred, the walk could be completed and tea taken in Burford which offers a choice of tea shop and is only a few minutes by car. Whilst the interior of the inn is quite small, there is a very large pleasant garden area extending down to the stream making it attractive to enjoy refreshments outdoors when the weather permits. Open from 11am and usual licensed hours. Tel: 01451 844385.

Description

The River Windrush is one of the best known of the small rivers which meander gently south east from the central part of the Cotswolds to join the River Thames near Oxford. South of Bourton-on-the-Water, the river valley is broad and shallow, with a few plantations of trees and the large Barrington deer park intruding into what would otherwise be a totally farming landscape.

Each of the three villages included in this walk has its own distinctive character. Great Barrington extends along both sides of a long street, with its church tucked into the near end of the deer park. A lofty Norman chancel arch and a memorial sculpted in marble to two children of the Bray family who died of smallpox in 1720 are the most striking features. Most of the church is of the 15th century.

Little Barrington is situated on the other side of the Windrush, grouped attractively around its sloping and rough-surfaced green. The church, away to the east of the village centre, is, again, largely of the 15th century but with a good Norman doorway inside the porch and a Norman tympanum in the north wall.

The small, picture postcard village of Windrush is close by, again to the south of the Windrush. Here, the 17th century corn mill is on the route of the walk. The church, by the side of the tiny green, is very substantially Norman.

Little Barrington

The Walk

Walk away from the church, down the road, turning right by the telephone box into a cul de sac road which soon loses its surface. Rise quite sharply to an old stone stile, ignore a wooden stile, and bend left

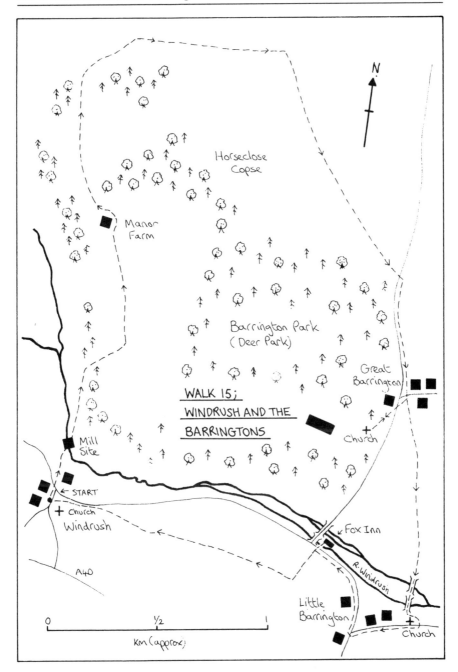

Horseclose Copse

Manor Farm

Barrington Park (Deer Park)

WALK 15;
WINDRUSH AND THE
BARRINGTONS

Great Barrington

Church

Mill Site

START

Church
Windrush

A40

Fox Inn

R. Windrush

Little Barrington

Church

0 .... ½ 1
Km (approx)

to another (rather awkward) stone stile. Go down a few steps to a sunken lane and turn right to the former Windrush Mill.

This is a very old mill site, with a fair proportion of the river passing under the building, where the water-wheel was obviously housed. Turn left to a farm gate/stile and follow the blue arrowed gates through the water meadows. A right turn at a gate part way along the boundary of a meadow leads up a slight rise to a well-defined track along the edge of a field, turning left to follow the top edge of the field straight towards Manor Farm, with its impressive farm house.

Follow the arrows round the farm, to the right, and continue along the broad track. At a "T" junction turn right to rise along the edge of a cultivated field, bending left at the next huge field (blue arrow). At the next intersection of paths and bridle ways, with several arrows, turn right. With the exception of one field, the broad track stays generally along the edges, always obvious.

Join the public road just to the north of Great Barrington, by the corner of the Barrington Park estate. Turn right to descend to Great Barrington village. At the road junction by the war memorial, a left turn is necessary to visit most of the village. To visit the church continue down the road and turn right in a short distance.

The main route continues from the war memorial into a lane to the right of a well-proportioned old house. The lane descends the Windrush valley side to a gate, then continues as a more open track to a former mill site by the river. Pass along the front of the buildings to a wooden footbridge and stile, and a well-used track across a water meadow. Another footbridge crosses the main part of the river, as Little Barrington is reached.

To see the church, turn left after the bridge and then rise to the right to reach the public road. Turn right at the top and walk along to the village green.

For a short cut to the green, turn right, along a footpath, after the bridge

At the green, turn right, downhill, along the road for a quarter of a mile. The Fox Inn, with its enticing outside terraces by the river and an ornamental pond, is on the right, just below a road junction.

From the inn return to the road junction and go straight across, to the left of a bus shelter. Two posts mark the position of a long defunct gate, Go through, under the spreading low branches of a horse chestnut tree, and follow the edge of a field. As the hedge ends, continue the same line past a small copse until a more obvious path from Little Barrington village to Windrush is joined. Turn right.

The way to Windrush continues over a stile, on the same line, with a good view of the splendid house at Barrington Park. The solidly squat tower of Windrush church comes into view ahead, with a farm below to the right. Keep well to the left of the farm, over several rudimentary stiles and through the odd gate with muddy areas, now heading right for the village. Bear left behind a house with a prominent conservatory before joining the road at a kissing gate to the right of the church. Turn left to return to the village centre.

A considerably shorter version of the above walk results from taking a right turn at Windrush Mill on to a footpath which joins the road between Windrush and Little Barrington. Turn left, then left again to pass the Fox Inn and reach Great Barrington along the road. From Great Barrington the route is as set out above.

16. Bourton-on-the-Water and Wyck Rissington

Length: 4½ miles

Summary: A generally level and easy circular walk from the quiet village of Wyck Rissington to the understandably popular large village of Bourton-on-the-Water, with its multiplicity of visitor attractions. En route are the lakes to the south-east of Bourton, an unusual part of the Cotswold landscape, and Salmonsbury Camp, an important lowland iron age fort. Apart from a little mud, there are no problems underfoot, although by no means all the tracks are visible on the ground.

Car Parking: At the south end of Wyck Rissington village a wide unmade farm track joins the public road at a corner. There is adequate parking space beside the track. Grid reference 191213.

Map: Ordnance Survey landranger no. 163, Cheltenham and Cirencester area.

Tea Shop

Bourton-on-the-Water has many tea shops. Having found the Bo-peep Tea Rooms listed in The Tea Council's Guide, this seemed the obvious choice. This café has won one of the Tea Council's awards of excellence each year from 1992.

There is a choice of at least seventeen varieties of tea, including gunpowder green, and Nilgiri, plus about eighteen choices of fruit tea, as well as herbal infusions. Leaf teas (no tea bags here) are used and are graded from 1 through to 8 according to strength. One could return time and time again to experiment with different varieties and permutations. If preferred, semi-skimmed milk, or slices of lemon are readily available upon request. Coffee and a range of other beverages are on the menu, as well as milk-shakes.

Food choices include clotted cream teas, Danish pastries, toasted tea cakes, sandwiches, cakes. Should an old-fashioned high tea be preferred, meals such as chicken, sausages, or plaice are all served with chipped potatoes.

The building itself is very old – probably dating from the 17th

Bourton-on-the-Water

century. The atmosphere is cosy with wood panelled walls and dark wood furniture. Open every day 10.30am – 5pm (extended to 6pm in summer and even later during peak periods). Tel. 01451 822005.

Description

The wide valley of the River Windrush has Bourton-on-the-Water and Burford as its best known settlements. The former sits on level ground, fringed by flooded gravel pits to the south-east which add an unusual, almost Norfolk broads, element to the landscape. The much smaller and quieter village of Wyck Rissington is linear in shape, bisected by a minor road which rises to climb the east side of the Windrush valley.

Bourton-on-the-Water is a most attractive village, particularly at quiet times, with the lawn and tree lined river running alongside the main street, crossed by numerous small bridges. Not entirely concealed by the modern manifestations of tourism are some fine old buildings, including a much rebuilt Manor House in High Street, an old mill, and two dovecotes.

The Roman Foss Way (now A429) crosses the Windrush on the edge of Bourton. Even earlier, possibly 3rd century BC, Salmonsbury Camp was constructed as an Iron Age fort, with ramparts and ditches surrounding a number of wooden huts. On this lowland site, swamps would make a considerable contribution to the overall defences of the fort.

Visitor attractions in Bourton include the famous model village – Bourton at a scale of one ninth, behind the Old New Inn (open all the year), Birdland (open all the year), Cotswold Motor Museum and Toy Collection (open February to November), Model Railway (open April to September), Village Life Exhibition (open February to November), Cotswold Perfumery (open all the year).

Apart from attractive houses, at Wyck Rissington most interest focuses on the parish church where, as a 17-year-old, Gustav Holst had his first professional post as organist. Outside, a living cross has been formed from a yew tree and there is an unusual headstone on the grave of a gypsy "of no fixed abode". Unfortunately, the celebrated maze in the garden beside the church is not at present open to the public.

The Walk

Set off along the wide farm trackway. When this track ends rather abruptly, turn right at a gate with a blue (bridleway) arrow. Keep to the edge of the field to reach an arrowed farm gate in the bottom left corner. Turn left here and cross a grassy meadow to an obvious gap.

The visible track now goes from gate to gate along the bottom edge of meadows, with Little Rissington church coming into view high on the left. Turn right at a neat stony driveway, leading to Rissington Mill, now a substantial residence. Take a marked stile on the left, to pass around the former mill, by a kissing gate, a footbridge over the mill tail race, with a weir on the right, then another bridge, crossing the River Eye.

The route continues along the side of the river, by a stile/gate, and across a long but narrow meadow, now being well-established and marked. Pass between small lakes attractively fringed by reeds and other rich vegetation, more typical of the Norfolk Broads.

On reaching a wide, unsurfaced, roadway, turn left to reach a lane with footpath signs. Turn right along the lane, to pass a cemetery before joining the public road. There is a short length of footpath on the left which cuts off a corner. Turn left to Bourton village centre. The tea shop described below is on the far side of the river.

To return to Wyck Rissington retrace the route along the main road to the junction with the lane, but carry on along the road for a few yards

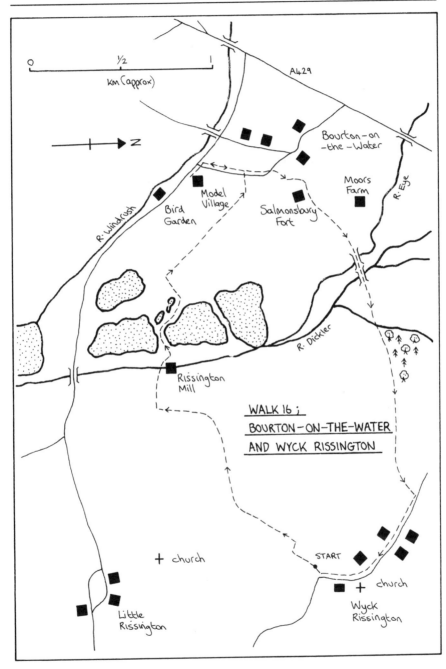

O ⊢————————————⊣
       ½
   km (approx)

⊢———⊢——▶ N

A429

Bourton-on-the-Water

R. Windrush

Moors Farm

R. Eye

Model Village

Bird Garden

Salmonsbury Fort

R. Dickler

Rissington Mill

WALK 16 ;
BOURTON-ON-THE-WATER
AND WYCK RISSINGTON

✝ church

START

✝ church

Wyck Rissington

Little Rissington

to Roman Way, where a sign points to "Wyck Rissington, Oxfordshire Way". Take the first right turn, Moor Lane, In a short distance after the last house on the right, turn right to ascend a few not too obvious stone steps with a stile at the top.

Take a clearly trodden path through the disturbed ground, part of Salmonsbury Camp. Continue along the edge of a field to a gate/stile, cross a lane to a very old kissing gate, and follow the same line, with the hedge on the left, thick with bramble. Two lifting barriers guard a wooden bridge over the River Eye, followed by a bridge over the River Dicker, with squeezer stiles. Cross a third bridge, over a stream.

Go straight on over the brow of the field beyond to two gates and a bridge, then bend left as indicated by an arrow, heading slightly uphill and to the left of the now visible village. Join the road at the north-west end of Wyck Rissington and walk up through the village, passing the spacious tree-lined green and the duckpond before reaching the church and then the parking place.

17. Upper and Lower Slaughter

Length: 3 miles

Summary: A short and easy circuit which visits both of these favourite villages, using a mixture of good footpaths and minor road. The initial ascent from Upper Slaughter is not too strenuous.

Car Parking: Small area close to the middle of Upper Slaughter. Grid reference 156232.

Map: Ordnance Survey Landranger no. 163, Cheltenham and Cirencester area.

Tea Shop

Unfortunately, at the time of writing neither of these famous Cotswold villages has a tea shop – very remiss. However, refreshments can be obtained at the Old Mill in Lower Slaughter. Each day, good quality pre-packed sandwiches are delivered; cold drinks are available and also delicious home-made dairy ice cream – try the unusual champagne and meringue or the more conventional strawberry.

Nicholas Granger and his partner purchased the mill in 1995 and have plans to open the Barn Tea Room sometime during 1996. For up-to-date information tel. 01451 820052.

Description

Both the Slaughters must rank among the best loved Cotswold villages. Sharing the gentle valley of the River Eye, which pursues its leisurely course to join the River Dicker at nearby Bourton-on-the-Water, they seem to epitomise all that the visitor expects of a Cotswold village.

Upper Slaughter is comparatively unspoilt, with the river crossed by a ford and tiny bridge. Close by are a dovecote, and a fine church much modified from its Norman origins. F.W. Witts, author of "The Diary of a Cotswold Parson" was rector here. A little way upstream is Eyford Park. Downstream, the original Manor House is largely Elizabethan and is regarded as one of the finest in the Cotswolds.

Lower Slaughter is much more of a visitor honeypot, with waterside former mill, immaculate golden stone cottages, little bridges over the river, and riverside greens all contributing to some of the most photo-

Mill at Lower Slaughter

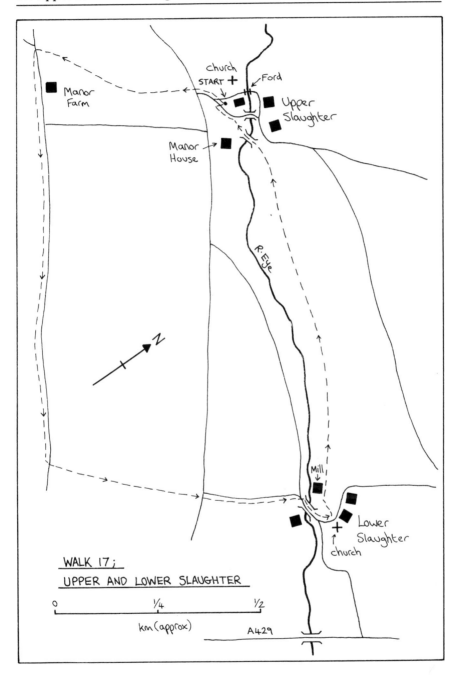

Church
START ✛
Ford
Manor
Farm
Upper
Slaughter
Manor
House
R. Eye
Z
Mill
Lower
Slaughter
church ✛

WALK 17;
UPPER AND LOWER SLAUGHTER

0   ¼   ½
km (approx)   A429

graphed scenes in Britain. The former 19th century corn mill still has its water wheel and is now in use as a museum, with associated shop. (open daily throughout the year).

The Walk

From the car park, turn right, uphill, to a "T" junction. Cross the road and go through a farm gate to a sunken lane heading up the hillside. Make for a farm gate at the top right hand corner of the field and bend right following the line indicated by an arrow. Manor Farm, now largely converted to industrial and trading units, is on the left.

On reaching the public road, turn left to continue for almost one mile. Turn left off the road, at a part concealed "Bridleway" sign, into a very obvious track, heading downhill, with the odd glimpse of Lower Slaughter below. Bourton-on-the-Water is visible to the right. Go straight across a public road and descend to Lower Slaughter, reaching the village opposite the famous mill.

After walking round the village, leave by a track behind the mill, part of the Warden's Way, through two kissing gates, the second of which records, now rather sadly, the "Marriage of Prince Charles and Lady Diana, 29th July, 1981".

Initially, the former mill ponds are alongside this pleasant and well-used track. With good waymarking, the route is never in doubt, passing Upper Slaughter Manor, away on the left, before descending to cross the river on a little footbridge. At the public road turn right to descend again to the river, cross the bridge, and turn left to reach the ford and old footbridge.

Cross yet again to climb back towards the car parking area. The church is set back to the right behind what appears to be the former school house. Note the bell!

18. Northleach and Hampnett

Length: 4½ miles

Summary: An easy circuit, predominantly using well-established tracks over farmland, based on the fine little town of Northleach. No real ascent and minimal roadside walking.

Car Parking: Market Square or The Green, in the middle of Northleach. Grid reference 114146.

Map: Ordnance Survey Landranger no. 163, Cheltenham and Cirencester area.

Tea Shop

The Corner Green Tea Shop is most attractive. The decor is delightful with a polished flag floor, dark Windsor style furniture, pretty curtains, navy blue table-cloths and matching crockery.

Food offered includes breakfast, which is actually available all day, as indeed is everything on the menu. Savouries include toasted sausage sandwiches, cheese muffins, smoked mackerel salad, quiche, plaice and chipped potatoes. There is, of course, a good range of items suitable for afternoon tea. Drinks to choose include various teas, coffee, Horlicks, or Bovril. The menu is extensive, with a separate list provided for children. Please note that on Sundays a traditional roast luncheon is served and reservations are advisable.

Open 10am – 5pm seven days each week from Easter to end of August but closed on Mondays for the remainder of the year. Note: always closed for three weeks in November. Tel. 01451 860240.

Description

Although situated close to the geographical centre of what is generally regarded as "the Cotswolds", there is a surprisingly remote, off the beaten track, feel about Northleach, by-passed by two of the great Cotswold highways, the A429 Foss Way and the A40.

Like most other small towns of the district, Northleach was a market town early in the 13th century (charter of 1227 granted by King Henry III), soon becoming a wealthy woollen town and, from the mid-16th century, a declining woollen town, as the rigid local guilds failed to move with the times and Stroud gradually emerged as the centre of the trade. However, unlike some other small towns, the industrial revolution and the 20th century influx of tourists en masse both passed Northleach by, leaving the town, despite its modern attractions, as a relatively undisturbed backwater.

Northleach

The parish church of St Peter and St Paul is dominant. One of the three great Cotswold "woollen churches" (the others are at Chipping Camden and Cirencester – see walks nos. 6 and 21), it was financed from the wealth accumulated by a handful of local woollen merchants. Built in the 15th century on the site of a previous church it is equally fine both inside and out. Of particular interest is the collection of memorial brasses, almost all to woollen merchants, said to be the finest in England. The importance of the humble sheep, as the source of local wealth, is recognised by its appearance on several brasses. Most also depict the woolpack. The collection is well-documented inside the church. The pulpit is noteworthy and, outside, there is a splendid porch.

The town was laid out by the Abbey of Gloucester around the triangular Market Place, with 80 burgage plots of equal size, to both north and south. Despite some later combination of the plots, the medieval layout is still apparent from a high viewpoint. There are many surviving historic buildings, including some of the twenty or so inns which catered for passing travellers and, presumably, a considerable local thirst.

The prison on the edge of town was built in 1790 by Sir George Onesiphorous Paul, who had a keen interest in penal reform. The prison was very advanced for its time, with exercise yards, baths and medical care. The building now houses the "Cotswold Countryside Collection – a museum of rural life". (open to the public daily from April to October). Back in town, "Keith Harding's World of Mechanical Music" is at the Oak House in High Street. (open daily except on Christmas Day).

Hampnett is also off the beaten track, a quiet farming hamlet by the headwaters of the River Leach. Its chief claim to fame is the extraordinary painting of the interior walls when the Norman/15th century church was restored in 1868. However, in marvelling at the boldness of the decoration, don't overlook two fine Norman arches at the east end and the low Norman vaulting of the sanctuary roof.

The Walk

From the Market Square, leave Northleach along High Street, lined with a rich and varied array of Cotswold stone buildings, including several of the archetypal gable fronted cottages, to reach the main A429 Foss Way by the traffic lights. Opposite is the former prison, interesting, but certainly not the prettiest of buildings.

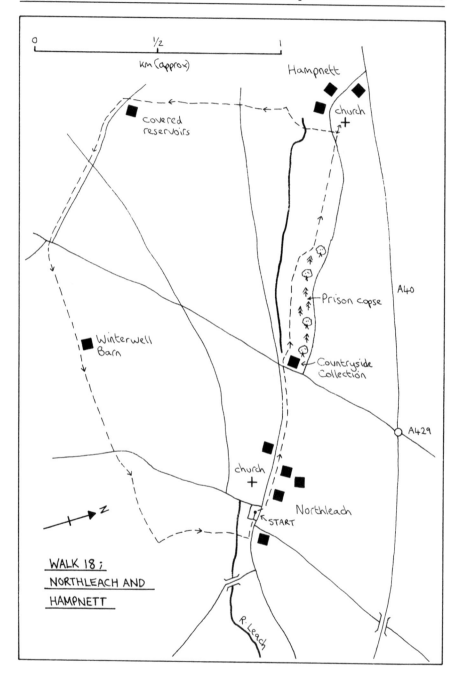

WALK 18;
NORTHLEACH AND
HAMPNETT

Cross the road and, in 20 yards, turn right over a stile with footpath sign. A well-marked track goes along the edge of the field and along the bottom of a shallow valley. Not surprisingly, the woodland across the field to the right is called Prison Copse. The tiny stream on the left is, believe it or not, the infant River Leach.

At a point where the obvious route ahead has been blocked by a farmer's fence, turn right to a stile with arrow at the edge of the woodland above. Go over the stile and follow the wall along the top of the meadow, rising a little. At the next stile, the arrow points straight across a cultivated field, where the path may or may not be restored. Go straight ahead boldly towards Hampnett. At the far end of this section, a decrepit kissing gate with signpost gives access to the public road. However, should courage fail, or the field be knee deep in mud, turn right by the stile, go through a farm gate, and turn left at the public road, leading directly to Hampnett.

From the church, return a few yards and turn right down a concreted farm roadway with a "public path" post. Pass a pond as the track bends right and loses its surface, now very close indeed to the source of the River Leach. In a further 200 yards, turn left at a junction and climb to a farm gate. Continue to rise towards a minor road, reached at another farm gate.

Go straight across to a bridleway and carry on over extensive flat upland, the broad track keeping to the right hand edge of a very large field, eventually reaching two covered reservoirs and another road. Turn left along the road, which is very quiet, soon reaching a crossroads. If you really do object to any form of roadside walking, there is a track along the edge of the field behind the roadside plantation on the right which avoids this quarter of a mile or so of road.

Go straight across at the crossroads and continue to the A429 Foss Way. Cross this major road to a gate with yellow arrow and a "public path" sign, and go along the edge of another huge field, then through the Winterwell Farm farm complex and along the access driveway. Cross yet another minor road and follow a signposted broad and potentially muddy trackway for about a quarter of a mile. Turn left at the end of a wall (yellow arrow) and follow the clear track towards Northleach, with a fine view of the town from this slightly elevated position.

After a stile, slant a little right, downhill, across a meadow, aiming just right of a tennis court. Go through a small gate by the side of a children's play area, alongside the tennis court, and cross the River Leach for the last time, before Meadow Lane leads back to the main street. Turn left to return to the Market Square.

19. Bibury and Quenington

Length: 8 miles

Summary: A varied circular walk, without any serious ascent, visiting villages both well known and not so well known, traversing what is arguably the best part of the valley of the River Coln. Underfoot, some muddy sections of footpath and some lengths of minor road, both in Quenington village and on the return route.

Car Parking: Small roadside parking area in Bibury, quite close to Arlington Mill. Grid reference 114068.

Map: Ordnance Survey Landranger no. 163, Cheltenham and Cirencester area.

Tea Shop

Arlington Mill is now restored to working order. Further plans are underway to repair the wheel and to make the machinery water-powered once again. Meanwhile the soothing noise and observation of the working cog-wheels gives a relaxing atmosphere whilst one partakes of well-earned refreshments.

The menu includes "Arlington Cream Tea" with sultana scones, clotted cream and jam, home-made cakes, filter coffee, choice of tea including Darjeeling, Assam, Earl Grey and herbal. Also available are light meals especially Bibury smoked trout (the trout farm is just next door). Try the terrace by the mill stream – lovely to sit here on a pleasant summer afternoon whist enjoying perhaps iced tea or coffee.

Special craft events are held in the mill during the summer months. There is a selection of gifts to purchase and bric-a-brac is also on display. Open 10am – 6pm daily from Easter to Christmas Eve. Tel. 01285 740368.

Description

Bibury, situated just a few miles to the north east of Cirencester, is one of the well known names of the Cotswolds, having been declared by William Morris to be the most beautiful village in England. The River Coln is crossed by a fine old bridge and is bounded by wide open grassy space in the village centre, with a large "island" created by the river and the tail race from nearby Arlington Mill. Rack Island is in the care of the National Trust and was formerly used for hanging cloth on oak racks after the fulling process had been carried out. It is now a protected area for water fowl breeding.

The real village centre is the close cluster of buildings around the parish church of St Mary, a little way downstream. Although rebuilt by the monks of Osney in the 13th century, this church is noted for the exceptional Saxon remains; some of the original work has been removed to the British Museum and been replaced by casts in Bibury. By the church is the 17th century Bibury Court, now a hotel.

Although now regarded as one place, strictly, Bibury is on the left bank of the river, whilst the village (or hamlet) of Arlington is on the right bank. The latter has the celebrated Arlington Row, beautiful former weavers' cottages owned by the National Trust, which must have provided the inspiration for a million biscuit and chocolate box lids. There is also Arlington Mill, a 17th century structure on a site which is mentioned in the Domesday Book. Used over the years both as a corn mill and as a cloth mill, it has been restored and now houses a museum of country crafts and, of course, our tea room. The mill is open to the public daily from Easter to Christmas Eve.

Close to the mill are a trout farm open to visitors and the 18th century Swan Hotel. A little way up the hill is the post office/store.

The River Coln at Bibury

In contrast to this wealth of interest for visitors, Quenington is hardly known. A straggling village, with quite nondescript development at the near end, it improves with progress along the street descending to the river, with two modest inns on the way. At the bottom is the real gem, the parish church with Quenington Court beside. The church is largely Norman, with carved stones set into the walls and, above all, two of the best Norman doorways in the whole of the Cotswolds, each being accompanied by a splendid tympanum and having a wealth of decorative carving. The Court has an old dovecote and a gatehouse which belonged to the Knights Hospitallers.

Coln St Aldwyns is a more conventionally attractive village than Quenington, having yet another fine church with Norman doorway and other features, and an Elizabethan manor house overlooking the river.

The Walk

From Arlington Mill, take the footpath opposite, signposted to Arlington Row, along the edge of Rack Island, soon reaching the famous terrace of cottages. Cross the river by a very old bridge, turning right at the main road, then right again towards the church. After the church, rise gently back to the main road, turn right, then right again in a short distance to take the minor road towards Coln St Aldwyns.

Turn right yet again in 50 yards down a surfaced little road with a bridleway sign. On the right the fine old house of Bibury Court is well seen across the lawns. Cross the river and bear right, uphill, through the Court Farm complex which, on the evidence of weir and sluices, to say nothing of displayed stones, must have included the site of a water powered mill. The roadway soon loses its surface, but remains an excellent broad track rising into woodland.

At the top of the rise, through a gate, turn left (blue arrow) and go straight on at another junction in 250 yards, keeping to the upper edge of woodland on a broad, possibly muddy track. Go straight on at a gate, now over grass along the bottom edge of a large field, before a steep little descent among young trees. At the bottom there is a choice of stile or gate. Angle left across a meadow to follow a faint path on the ground to a gate and stile with a warning notice and advice about adders.

Continue, generally close to the river, through a small wood, then along the foot of a sloping field as the river meanders to the left. Pass a curiously hollow tree, part of an old hedgerow. Where wheel tracks turn sharp right, keep straight on through a gate, then bend right, away from the river, at a footpath sign, rising a little towards woodland. Follow an

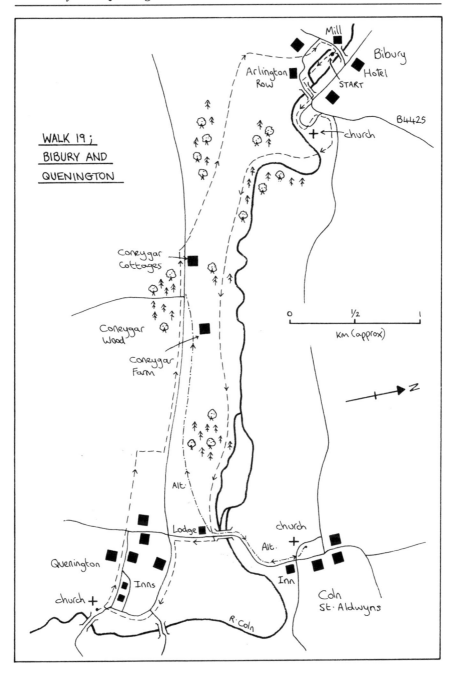

old wall along the bottom edge of the wood before entering the wood on a broad track, soon reaching a gate giving access to an open meadow, with yet another warning about adders, surely not common in riverside meadowland? Could this, in fact, be a not very subtle deterrent for the less than determined walker?

Coln St Aldwyns village is now close on the left and the public road is reached at Yew Tree Lodge.

Turn left here for a detour to visit Coln St Aldwyns.

For a direct return to Bibury, follow the obvious track, signposted as a bridleway, rising to the left from the gate behind Yew Tree Lodge. In just over one mile across farmland this track rejoins the recommended circuit at the minor road, close by the isolated roadside Coneygar Cottages.

To proceed to Quenington, which is highly recommended (you could, of course, cheat by short cutting the walk and driving to Quennington after refreshment) turn right, up the road, rising quite steeply. Turn left at the road junction at the top of the rise, to follow Fowlers Hill, which bends to the right to join the main village street, Church Road, in about half a mile. Turn left to descend to the river and the church, nicely set among good Cotswold buildings, including Quenington Court.

Return along Church Road past two inns, the Earl Grey being a particularly tiny free house, to the village green. Like this upper end of Quenington generally, the surroundings of the green are less than enchanting. Go straight across to a public footpath sign, to the left of a terrace of houses, and take the surfaced roadway. By the entrance to "Mallards", take the walled track on the right, leading to a stile in a few yards. Continue along the edge of a large field, then turn right at a rudimentary stile in less than a quarter of a mile, heading directly for the public road, reached at a gate/stile by a cattle-churned area.

Turn left to follow the quiet road for just over one mile. Approximately 150 yards after passing Coneygar Cottages, turn right at a footpath sign into an unsurfaced lane, becoming a farm track, always obvious as it descends to a grassy bottom and then rises along the right hand edge of woodland before crossing a large expanse of upland farm land. On reaching a junction with blue and yellow arrows, turn right to follow the blue arrow along another good track, soon reaching the edge of Arlington/Bibury. As the path divides, go straight ahead to a post festooned with footpath signs. Go through the small gate to reach an unmade roadway and the public road.

Turn left to reach a more important road and then right to descend past the village post office/stores to Arlington Mill.

20. Cotswold Water Park

Length: 6 miles

Summary: A level circuit around part of the Cotswold Water Park, using the towpath of a disused canal and an abandoned railway line for much of the way, visiting the substantial village of South Cerney and the hamlet of Cerney Wick. Easy to follow, well-used paths throughout, with almost one mile of minor road in South Cerney.

Car Parking: Spacious public car park, with public conveniences and information facilities on the Spine Road, a quarter of a mile from the junction of that road with the main A419, Swindon to Cirencester road. Grid reference 072971.

Map: Ordnance Survey Landranger no. 163, Cheltenham and Cirencester area.

Tea Shop

The Samuel Pepys Coffee Shop in South Cerney appears to be the only tea shop in The Cotswold Water Park. The lack of this kind of facility encouraged the owners of The Eliot Arms to open this most attractive room, with its own entrance door, at one end of the hotel. It has a pleasant forecourt, with tables and chairs placed here in the summer months whilst in December the Christmas tree looked very festive and was appropriately set against this lovely old building.

A choice of coffee is available and is served in cafetières. Also a variety of teas are offered plus scones, biscuits and cakes. If you wish to "convert" to high-tea you will be welcome to add something from the very extensive menu which is available all day and ranges from ploughman's lunches to healthy salads, all-day breakfast (not available on Sundays!) to sandwiches and even chip butties!

The decor is very pleasing, the service hospitable, and walkers are always made very welcome. Evening meals are served in the main hotel and accommodation with en-suite facilities is available.

Coffee Shop open 10am – 5pm all the year. Tel. 01285 860215.

Description

The numerous lakes of the Cotswold Water Park cover a large area about

South Cerney tea shop

five miles to the south of Cirencester. Extensive former Thames valley gravel workings, started more than 60 years ago, have been flooded to form the Park, now used for a variety of leisure activities, including several forms of boating. Whilst, inevitably, there are still raw edges, the landscape has settled down well and the area as a whole is surprisingly attractive, with both public and private nature reserves, and national importance as a wildlife habitat. A range of information boards at the recommended car park outlines the history, the leisure uses, and the flora and fauna of the Park. The River Thames flows through the western end of the lakes.

South Cerney is a large straggling settlement of largely modern development. At the core, however, is an old Cotswold village, with several 17th century houses in Silver Street. Despite later additions, the church has plenty of surviving Norman features, notably the tower and two doorways. A carved stone plaque over the south door is believed to be Saxon, presumably taken from some earlier church. Among many internal features of interest are two fragments of a 12th century carved wood crucifix, claimed to be the oldest surviving piece of carved wood in the country.

The Thames and Severn Canal is briefly mentioned in walk no. 26. The section to the south east of Cirencester is a wholly delightful rural waterway, with the occasional ruined lock and one of the rare and distinctive "round house" canal employee's dwellings at Cerney Wick.

The Midland and South West Junction Railway was one of those cross country railways which, from the outset, were never likely to be really successful, but which are widely remembered with great nostalgia. Perhaps the Somerset and Dorset was the epitome of this kind of railway. Completed as a through line as late as 1883, the M. & S.W.J ran from its junction with a minor line at Andoversford, a few miles east of Cheltenham, to a connection with the main line of the London and South Western Railway at Andover, a classic case of starting and finishing at nowhere in particular. Although the development of Salisbury Plain as a great military training area did give a considerable boost, and there were particularly busy spells during both world wars, the only places of consequence along the line were Swindon, already well-served as the headquarters of the mighty Great Western, and Cirencester. Somehow the line managed to keep its independent status until the grouping of 1922/3, when it was absorbed by the Great Western. Unfortunately but inevitably, it could not survive the widespread closures of uneconomic lines in the 1960s.

The Walk

From the car park, turn right along the road and then right again in a few yards, through a squeezer stile and down a few steps. The footpath sign is to "Cerney Wick 1". Fork left immediately to follow the towpath of the former Thames and Severn Canal, a delightful stroll, reaching a minor road in about one mile. Close to the road are a lock and a most interesting canal lengthsman's round house.

Turn right along the road into Cerney Wick, crossing the River Churn before reaching the Crown Inn. At the road junction go straight ahead over a stile signposted to Ashton Keynes, crossing a tiny meadow, then a minor road. Go straight on, along the edge of meadows, over stiles and a wooden walkway (yellow arrow) to reach a lake.

Follow the defined path, bending right then left. Sixty yards after the left bend look out for a yellow arrow and turn left down a few steps to a squeezer stile, bridge, and odd little gate. Continue to the trackbed of the former Midland and South West Junction Railway line. Away to the left a high brick bridge carrying a road over the railway can be seen.

Turn right at the signpost "South Cerney 1½ miles", only one mile

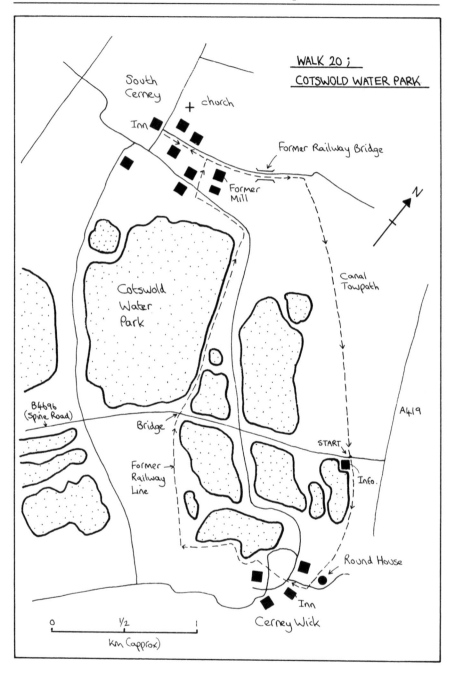

away from the River Thames at this point. The trackbed makes a first class walking surface as it runs straight and level to the main (Spine) road. Cross the road and go under a remarkable brick bridge with unusual piers which carried the original road over the railway line. There is an observation point on the top of this bridge.

Continue along the trackbed, signposted "South Cerney lakes" now effectively a causeway between lakes. Across the water, to the right, is a spick and span development of lakeside (holiday?) homes. Turn left as a public road is joined, approaching South Cerney. As this becomes Station Road, the site of the former station will not be too difficult to identify.

Continue towards the centre of the spacious village. Just after the junction with Lennards Road, turn right to take a surfaced footpath along the backs of properties, reaching the side of the River Churn by Lower Mill. Either cross the bridge and turn left to follow the roadway to the main road and the Elliot Arms *or* turn left over a stile before the bridge to take an ill-defined field edge footpath. As a house "Hideaway" is reached, go over a stile in the right hand corner of the field and, after a few yards along the bank of a mill head-race, cross a bridge and turn left to reach the main road in less than 100 yards, the Elliot Arms being directly opposite.

From the tea shop, cross the road and return along the roadway ("Bow Wow"!) opposite. This roadway, beautifully lined with willows, lies between the River Churn and the head-race of a former water mill. Pass Lower Mill, cross the river and rise over a former railway bridge. On reaching the course of the canal, turn right along the former towpath, signposted "Cerney Wick 2 miles".

Boxwell Spring lock, apparently partially reconstructed, is soon reached. Go over a stile and continue. As on the outward part of the walk, the old towpath makes an excellent route, good underfoot and foolproof to follow along the tree-lined banks of the long derelict canal. Lakes on the eastern extremity of this part of the water park come into view before the ruins of another lock and a demolished bridge are passed.

Below this point there is a little water in the trough of the canal. At the next lock, with bridge, considerable engineering works were found to be in progress. The ruin of a canalside cottage is visible on the far side. Go straight on at this junction of the ways, to the main (Spine) road and turn right to return to the car park.

21. Cirencester and Stratton

Length: 5 miles

Summary: Coupling Earl Bathurst's Cirencester Park land with an expanse of farming countryside, focused on the ancient town of Cirencester, this is an excellent, easy, circuit. Virtually no ascent, no complex route finding, and no mud or other difficulty underfoot.

Car Parking: From the junction of the two main roads, A417 and A433, drive towards Gloucester (A417). In a quarter of a mile approx. is a minor cul de sac on the left, followed by a similar cul de sac 300 – 400 yards further. Just a little further still is a minor road to Daglingworth. Each of these three roads provides opportunities for the careful parking of a vehicle off the main road. In the case of the Daglingworth road, park close to the cemetery. Grid references: 013034; 012038; 010040.

Map: Ordnance Survey Landranger no. 163, Cheltenham and Cirencester area.

Tea Shop

Oddly, it proved difficult to find a suitable venue for afternoon tea in this good-sized town. Once found, however, we can certainly recommend the Coffee House at the Brewery Arts Centre. It is counter-service here with a tempting display of unusual cakes, scones, chocolate and date flapjacks, Mars Bar shortbread slices etc. There is also a selection of salads and hot savouries. Drinks include a variety of teas, coffees, hot chocolate, citron pressé, and cranberry juice. The environment is pleasant – green painted furniture with tiled table tops, and paintings displayed on the walls available for purchase.

Open all the year, Monday to Saturday, 10am to 5pm. Tel. 01285 654791.

Description

Strategically placed in the centre of the Cotswold plateau, second city of England in Roman times, later with centuries of wool-derived prosperity, good stone buildings in abundance and a truly great church in the Market Place, Cirencester seems to have everything going for it. Even most of the through traffic is routed around the town . . . yet . . . somehow, despite all these advantages, the overall impression of the town is somewhat less than the expected sum of the various parts.

Cirencester Park

Despite the ring road, it must have something to do with the motor car. At seemingly all times of day, the town centre has huge areas covered by parked vehicles, no doubt useful for both shoppers and visitors but, coupled with the absence of pedestrianised streets, unquestionably detracting from the overall appeal of the town.

Having said that, Cirencester is still an interesting town, with the Corinium museum, traces of a Roman amphitheatre, Brewery Arts and much else to see, making a fine focal point for the present walk. The parish church is magnificent by any standards, largest of the celebrated Cotswold wool churches, with a great 15th century tower. The inside is a treasure house both in terms of the structure and of the possessions, which include, brasses, embroideries and the Boleyn Cup, a gilt cup made for Queen Anne Boleyn in 1535, which bears her family crest. Close to the church is the ancient market cross.

Stratton is a primarily residential outpost of Cirencester, occupying the V between the main roads to Gloucester and to Cheltenham.

The Walk

From the middle of the three suggested parking places, walk to the farm at the end of the road, turning right to follow a broad track signposted as a bridleway, soon rising gently to the left.

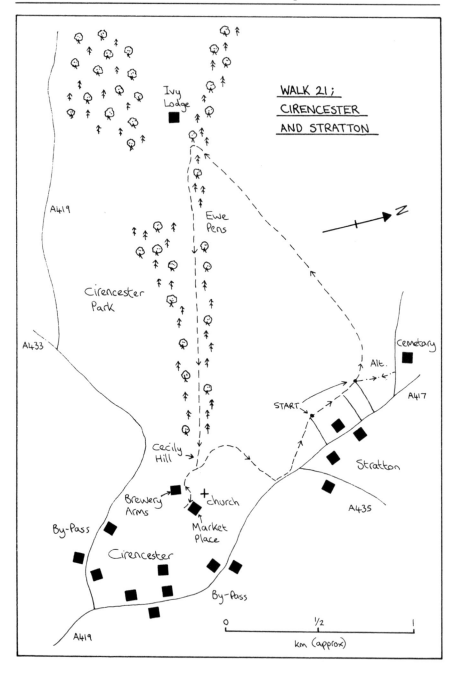

WALK 21;
CIRENCESTER
AND STRATTON

To reach the farm from the first parking place, take a signposted path by the side of allotment gardens and turn left on reaching the roadway. To reach the farm from a parking place near to the cemetery, cross the road to a footpath leading back in a very short distance to the roadway and turn right.

At a broken gate with yellow and blue arrows go straight ahead. The continuous track provides an excellent tramp across wide, open spaces for almost 1½ miles to Cirencester Park, keeping straight ahead at the only junction. As the park boundary is reached, note the conditions for the use of this privately owned land which are set out on a prominent blue notice board. Probably the least expected of these conditions is that which prohibits dogs.

Bend left to enter the park and turn left towards Cirencester. The choice now is between following a roadway, left, among attractive woodland or going ahead for a further 70-80 yards before turning left to walk over lush grass. In the latter case a polo field is passed, with right, then left, bends before resuming the straight line towards Cirencester.

For about 1½ miles the route follows a wide avenue between trees, heading straight for the tower of Cirencester church, presumably the alignment being intentional at the time the park was laid out. The alternative route on the parallel roadway joins this avenue about one third of the way along. Pass the park entrance lodge and gates and descend Cecily Hill. Turn right and then left along Black Jack Street to walk to the Market Place. For Brewery Arts and the tea shop go a few yards down Cricklade Street, opposite the church, and then turn right.

Leave Cirencester by returning to Cecily Hill, but pass the lower end of this street and, in a further 25 yards, turn left at a "riverside walk" sign. Pass the open air swimming pool, go straight across a minor road and cross the River Churn on a footbridge.

On reaching the main road, turn left. The roadside trackway is signposted as being also for the use of cyclists, so take care! Walkers will not wish to linger on this section, but it is mercifully short. Turn left at a gate opposite the major road junction, and then right at a kissing gate to take a path worn over the grass leading to a stile and driveway with houses. Straight ahead is the surfaced road which may, of course, be your parking place. If not, go across to a signposted gate and take the path by the side of the allotment gardens to the roadway which is the second recommended parking place. If you have parked by the cemetery, the final part of the return is along another short section of footpath ahead, leading to the Daglingworth road.

22. Tetbury

Length: 5 miles

Summary: A pleasant walk in the gently undulating countryside to the south and east of the delightful market town of Tetbury, crossing the park land of the Estcourt Estate, Shipton Wood, and visiting the isolated church at Long Newnton.

Car Parking: Substantial signposted car park, with public conveniences, to the north west of Tetbury town centre. Grid reference 887933.

Map: Ordnance Survey Landranger no. 173, Swindon, Devizes and surrounding area.

Tea Shop

There are numerous tea shops in Tetbury. We sampled The Gallery Tea Room, which is entered through a room with a small exhibition of paintings to add to the interest of the visit. Going into the tea room is like entering someone's home – small, cosy, and with friendly service.

Morning coffee is served, followed by light lunches with a choice of salads, soup, or, for something different, try a hot cheese scone with Cheddar cheese and Devon chutney.

In the afternoon temptations abound; items on offer are toasted crumpets with butter, toasted tea cakes and delicious, unusual varieties of cake, which are made on the premises. We tried the orange syrup cake which proved moist and more-ish! Good range of teas including, Assam, Lapsang, Earl Grey etc.

Open: 11am – 5.30pm every day; closed for Christmas from mid-December. Tel. 01666 503412.

Description

Situated less than three miles from the Gloucestershire/Wiltshire boundary, Tetbury is very much at the southern fringe of the district. Nevertheless, it is a real Cotswold town, stone built and tightly clustered around the former market hall of 1655, with the soaring slender spire of St Mary's church visible for miles around.

The town's long history inevitably includes prosperity as a woollen town but, unlike many others, Tetbury was never wholly dependant on wool, having greater diversity as a wide ranging market town, helped by having acquired its own manorial rights early in the 17th century.

St Mary's church was built on the site of an earlier church in Gothic style in 1781, with exceptionally large windows and a very unusual interior. This date is late by Cotswold standards, which must have something to do with the lack of local dominance by wealthy wool barons in the preceding four centuries.

Tetbury

There are many buildings worthy of note in the town; a stroll around the centre is highly recommended. Apart from the obvious market hall, "renovated" in 1817, there is the nearby 17th century Snooty Fox Inn, on the corner of Chipping Lane. This lane leads to the site of the original market – the "Chipping", with the medieval Chipping Steps going down from here towards the River Avon, and the fine house "The Croft" at the bottom. Close by, "The Priory" contains a small part of the old monastic buildings.

Most of today's excellent range of shops and refreshment places are housed in 17th and 18th century buildings, Long Street containing some particularly good examples. The coats of arms over several of the frontages emphasises the proximity of certain royal residences, notably that of the Prince of Wales at Highgrove House, less than two miles along the Westonbirt and Bath road. There is also a small museum of police bygones and a Tourist Information Centre.

Until 1964 there was a branch railway line from the junction at Kemble to a terminus in the valley immediately to the south east of the town centre.

Although since renovated, Long Newnton church still has a 15th century tower, with a prominent sundial. An avenue of beeches leads to the adjacent rectory.

The Walk

Leave Tetbury by the B4014 Malmesbury road, descending quite steeply from the town centre to a high bridge over a small stream, headwaters of the infant River Avon (Bristol). Look carefully at the valley on the left just after crossing the stream. With what looks like a former approach road, this must be the site of the terminus station of the long closed branch railway line, serviced by generations of modest former G.W.R. rolling stock, puffing sedately to and fro from the junction with the Gloucester to Swindon and Paddington line at Kemble.

Just after the bridge turn right to descend a broad trackway with a public footpath sign. Pass a cottage and, as the roadway bends left, go over a waymarked stile on the right. Follow the left arrow up to another stile and continue along the edge of a field, with a sewage works below to the left. The path is quite distinct as it leads from stile to stile. On reaching a farm gate, follow the arrows over two stiles, keeping much the same line. Slads Farm is visible to the left.

Turn right through a farm gate and descend rudimentary steps to a

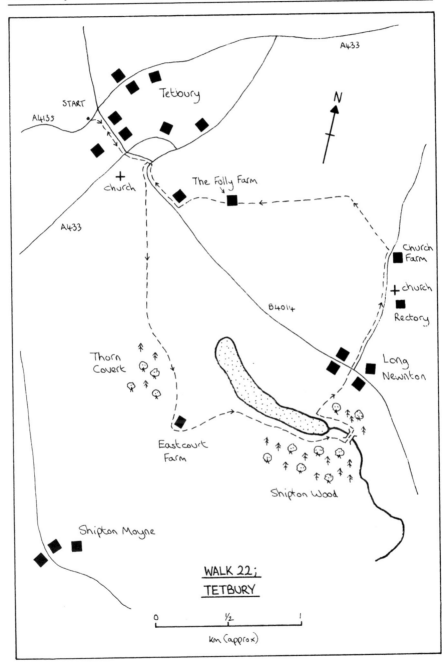

A433

Tetbury

START

A4135

church

A433

The Folly Farm

Church Farm

church

Rectory

B4014

Thorn Covert

Long Newiton

Eastcourt Farm

Shipton Wood

Shipton Moyne

WALK 22;
TETBURY

0   ½   1

km (approx)

N

stream. Cross two bridges to a stile and follow the direction indicated by the yellow arrow, to the left of Thorn Covert, ahead. As a surfaced driveway, part of the Estcourt Estate, comes into view, angle left towards a yellow arrow on a post. Join the driveway here to traverse very traditionally English park land.

Go straight ahead at a waymarked junction and turn left 20 yards after a cattle grid to follow a roadway among the many and varied buildings of Estcourt, which, despite the odd corrugated roof and some dilapidation, comprise a generally attractive complex of Cotswold architecture.

As the roadway bends left into a large yard, fork right along a broad track into light woodland. The track soon swings left, then right, with a pond now visible to the left. Keep left, slightly downhill, at a fork and continue along this very attractive part of the route, soon by the bottom edge of Shipton Wood, deciduous, including a great deal of oak.

The stream below widens out into more ponds. At a junction turn left to cross the stream on a bridge by the weirs which have obviously created the ponds above. Go straight on at a fork after the bridge, looping back to the left to reach a farm gate. The track across the narrow field ahead is just visible as it heads to a very tight and decrepit kissing gate. From here follow the edge of the fields to the public road by the straggling settlement of Long Newton.

Cross over to the minor road to head towards the church. To the left the slender spire of St Mary's church at Tetbury soon becomes visible. Long Newnton rectory, ahead, is a handsome, well-proportioned residence rather spoiled by its flat roof. The church is noted for its prominent sundial and for the mini avenue of beeches leading to the rectory.

Continue along the road, past a junction, to Church Farm beyond. Opposite the farm turn left through a farm gate with a footpath waymark. Follow the indicated direction across the field to a gate. Go through and continue the same line across the next field. However, this field might be found to be cultivated and the line of the path obliterated. In these circumstances, you might prefer to keep to the left hand boundary, then turning right at the far end to continue along that boundary.

In either case, reach a stile with yellow arrow and go over, crossing another cultivated field, now heading for the church spire and The Folly farm. Go through a farm gate and along a farm track to the muddy approach to the farm, traversed by a concrete roadway. At a complex of holiday cottages, turn left to join the public road, turning right to return to Tetbury.

23. Westonbirt

Length: 4 miles

Summary: An easy level walk circumnavigating the famous Arboretum, through the park land of Westonbirt School, along the farmland edge of the Arboretum, and then back to the Visitor Centre for refreshments. No doubt most walkers will wish to combine the walk with a visit to the Arboretum and/or the associated Silk Wood. Parts of the path may well be muddy.

Car Parking: Large car park serving the Arboretum. Grid reference 849898. Payment is required during the summer season.

Map: Ordnance Survey Landranger nos. 162, Gloucester and the Forest of Dean area; 173, Swindon, Devizes and surrounding area (either, as there is an overlap on these maps).

Tea Shop

This is a refreshment facility and certainly not a tea shop – it is open air and the crockery is of the disposable variety. The good news however is the lovely sheltered courtyard setting, clean, tidy, attractive and definitely different. As befits a Forestry Commission enterprise, the tables and benches are in natural wood with some areas attractively roofed-over to give protection from the weather. It is, therefore, quite possible to enjoy refreshments here on any day of the year, except perhaps in really severe conditions. During the Christmas period many people visit Westonbirt to purchase trees grown in the park (and perhaps to meet Father Christmas!) and one of these trees, suitably illuminated, forms the centre piece of the courtyard café during the festive period. The menu offers hot soup, tea, coffee, sandwiches (including hot bacon), wrapped biscuits, cakes etc. all at reasonable prices.

Open all the year during daylight hours. Tel. 01666 880220.

Description

The famous Arboretum at Westonbirt has 600 acres planted with 18,000 or so specimens, in fact one of the greatest collections of trees and shrubs in the world. With 17 miles of waymarked path, a comprehensive visitor centre, education centre, plant and other sales, it is deservedly popular for family excursions.

First planted in 1829 by Robert Holford, Westonbirt is certainly now a garden for all seasons, spectacular in spring with the azaleas and rhododendrons and in autumn, with the changing colour of the acers.

Westonbirt

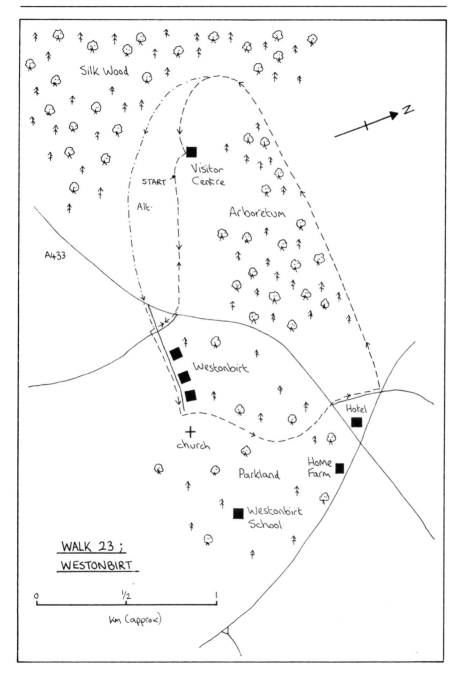

Silk Wood

Visitor
Centre

START

Alt.

A433

Arboretum

Westonbirt

Hotel

+ church

Parkland

Home
Farm

Westonbirt
School

WALK 23 ;
WESTONBIRT

0   ½   1

Km (approx)

The hamlet of Westonbirt was almost wholly rebuilt by Holford to the west of the 14th century parish church to give more space for gardens around his home, Westonbirt House, a huge Victorian mansion built in an Elizabethan style. It is now used as an independent school. The rebuilt hamlet has one straight street of wide spaced properties, with little variety of style or material to add interest.

The Walk

Head down the entrance drive back towards the main road. Cross over to the minor road opposite, signposted "Westonbirt village ¼", turn left at the next cross-roads and continue along the 19th century village street towards the church and golf course. An "old post office" and a long defunct village pump add just a little interest to the otherwise unremarkable scene.

At the end of the row turn left, over a cattle grid, at the entrance gate to a Westonbirt School private road. The church and the golf course are further along the road which continues ahead at this point. The school roadway crosses level park land, with the great house, now the school, well away to the right. At a "T" junction, go straight ahead, over grass, keeping much the same line along the edge of a plantation.

Bear away a little left of the trees to a farm gate/kissing gate and a potentially muddy area. From the gate bend left across a meadow without a visible path towards a farm gate with footpath sign giving access to the main road. Go straight across the road into a minor road.

At the approach to cross-roads, turn left over a stile with yellow arrow to follow a distinct path which holds a virtually straight line for more than a mile. A corner of the Arboretum is soon reached and the route then follows the boundary, along the edge of a succession of fields.

Eventually, at a farm gate with yellow arrow, enter the Arboretum grounds on a right of way and slant left, downhill, on a sunken grassy track across a park land section of the gardens. At the bottom of the slope turn left along the valley bottom towards a roadway. Follow the roadway back to the car park/visitor centre/tea shop.

Should no refreshment or visit to the arboretum be desired, and if car parking has been found elsewhere, the public bridleway may be followed through to the main road. In this case, do not rise to the roadway as above, but keep to the valley bottom, fairly close to the fence on the right, eventually reaching the road along an unsurfaced lane.

24. Wotton-under-Edge

Length: 6 miles

Summary: From the compact historic town of Wotton-under-Edge, this walk climbs steadily to the Tyndale Monument, perched on the fine viewpoint of Nibley Knoll. Much of the route is in attractive woodland, passing the iron age fort of Brackenbury. The tracks are clear and well used, with minimal roadside walking.

Car Parking: At "The Chipping", by the Heritage Centre/Tourist Information Office in Wotton-under-Edge. Grid reference 757932. Public conveniences are tucked away round the corner in Rope Walk, a pedestrian route to the main Street.

Map: Ordnance Survey Landranger no. 162, Gloucester and the Forest of Dean.

Tea Shop

There is a lovely friendly atmosphere in Wotton-under-Edge. Although on the Cotswold Way, this town is somewhat off the main track of the tourists and the Wotton Coffee Shop reflects the same character – homely and unsophisticated – although situated in one of the most attractive old buildings in the town. The sign outside states that ramblers are welcome. Coffee and tea is served by the cup, mug, or pot. A "breakfast special" is offered as well as bacon sandwiches, jacket potatoes, soup etc. In the afternoon Cotswold Cream Teas are served and home-made cakes are always available. Of particular interest to those walking the Cotswold Way, bed and breakfast is offered at this combined coffee shop and guest house.

Open 9am to 4.30pm each day (not Sundays or Bank Holiday Mondays and also closed Christmas week and New Year's Day). Tel. 01453 843158.

Description

Wotton-under-Edge really is under edge, nestling below the high escarpment well to the south west of the district. The town has a long history, in the early years closely linked with the Berkeley family whose castle is situated just a few miles away. After destruction by mercenary

Almshouses at Wotton-under-Edge

troops at the time of King John, it was rebuilt and became a market town, with borough status in 1252.

Inevitably in this area, the cloth trade assumed great importance and was largely responsible for the development of the town as seen today. As would be expected in an important woollen town, the parish church, of 13th century origin, is a fine structure with a great tower and a 15th century clerestory. Inside is a memorial brass to members of the Berkeley family and an organ constructed by Christopher Shrider for St Martin's in the Fields, London, during the reign of King George I. Handel played this organ at the opening. In 1800 it was put up for sale and was acquired by the then vicar of Wotton.

There are three well known groups of almshouses, probably the most interesting being the Perry and Dawes in Church Street, clustered around a little courtyard chapel, open to visitors. Other good historic buildings include the former Ram Inn, part 13th century, in Synwell Lane by the stream, the 17th century Berkeley House half way up Long Street, and Tolsey House, with the clock which commemorates the diamond jubilee of Queen Victoria. Wotton Grammar School was founded more than 600 years ago, one of the oldest in England, followed by the Bluecoat School in 1715.

Isaac Pitman was the master of the British School on the corner of Bear Lane when he worked on his invention of the shorthand system which bears his name. His house in Orchard Street has an appropriate plaque.

Modern Wotton has a good array of shops and the Heritage Centre (open daily, Tuesday to Saturday throughout the year and on the afternoon of the first Sunday in the month from June to October), with an intriguing collection of local material.

Brackenbury Camp is a triangular iron age hill fort of eight acres, skilfully using the natural contours of the Cotswold scarp. It is now largely obscured by trees but can readily be examined by a short detour from the route of this walk.

The Tyndale monument was erected on Nibley Knoll in 1866 in memory of William Tyndale, born nearby late in the 15th century. For the benefit of ordinary people he began the first translation of the New Testament into the English language in the early 1520s, completing his work abroad in 1526, after hostility in England. Having started work on the Old Testament, he was imprisoned, charged with heresy and executed in Flanders in 1538.

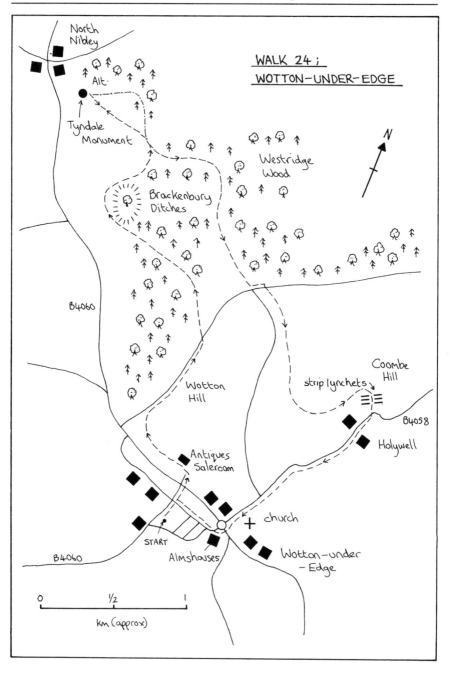

WALK 24;
WOTTON-UNDER-EDGE

North
Nibley

Alt·

Tyndale
Monument

N

Brackenbury
Ditches

Westridge
Wood

B4060

Coombe
Hill

strip lynchets

Wotton
Hill

B4058

Holywell

Antiques
Saleroom

church

START

B4060

Almshouses

Wotton-under
-Edge

0   ½   1

km (approx)

The Walk

Leave the car park along Market Street, by the side of the cinema. Turn left, uphill, along High Street for 60 yards, then turn right into Bear Street. Cross the main road and ascend Tabernacle Pitch, opposite. Bear left by the redundant church, now a well known auction centre, and rise steadily, keeping straight on along a path as the road peters out. The well used path between banks continues to rise until it joins a minor road beside a viewpoint with seat.

Turn right to continue uphill along the road. Ignore two obvious footpaths on the left, staying with the road until the crest of the rise is reached, by a lay-by. Turn left here into a signposted bridle way. Most of the hard work of the walk has now been done. The excellent track has a narrow belt of woodland to the left and a field to the right; at a junction of bridle ways keep left, now totally in varied deciduous woodland, rising almost imperceptibly.

At a major meeting place of tracks, fork left to follow a yellow arrow painted on a tree, slightly downhill. At the next fork, in about 40 yards, keep right along a level track which terraces around the hillside for some distance, with the tree covered Brackenbury fortifications above to the right, and splendid views to the left.

Suddenly, the Tyndale monument comes into view ahead, with a little more uphill work obviously required. At a meeting place of many tracks, take the obvious route slightly to the left, towards the monument, first with blue and then with yellow arrows. A track over the grass beside the fence on the left leads straight to the tower, a splendid piece of Victorian construction. A topograph which was erected by the people of North Nibley to commemorate the Silver Jubilee of Queen Elizabeth II details the more important features visible on a clear day, including Ozleworth Tower, Severn Bridge, Haresfield Beacon and Sugar Loaf mountain (1955 feet).

Entry to the tower is permitted, for a small charge, but the catch is that you have to pop down to North Nibley village – close by but several hundred feet down the steep scarp – for the key! A plaque on the monument gives brief details of Tyndale.

Return to the meeting place of many tracks, either by the outward route or, if variation is desired, with your back to the door of the monument, bearing a little left across the grass to a stile, then turning right. At the meeting place, go ahead, bending left, uphill, on a broad track which soon levels out to cross a more open area planted with young conifers.

For the first time, serious mud underfoot may be encountered here.

As the major track bends left by some mature trees, go straight on along a more minor track. Turn left as another major track is joined in a short distance, then right at the next junction, the woodland now being a mixture of deciduous and coniferous, with some unfortunate "straight line" planting on the left.

At another major meeting place of routes, bear a little right to take the track which has woodland to the left and a field on the right, leading to a farm type gate and the minor road. Turn left for a few yards, cross over, and leave the road over a stile signposted "public footpath Coombe Hill".

The narrow path soon joins a more important path. Turn right here and then fork right (yellow arrow) to descend through woodland to a gate/stile. The very fine path terraces around the flank of the hill for some distance, with gallery-like views of Wotton-under-Edge. As the path commences its ascent of Coombe Hill, look out for a right turn to two stiles.

Go over and cross the meadow to another stile giving access to the road, at the hamlet of Holywell. This meadow has a particularly well-marked series of strip lynchets, ancient cultivation terraces, through which the path passes. Turn right at the road and return to Wotton, with some not very appealing suburban views to the left, but the great solid tower of the parish church reassuringly ahead.

At the main road go straight across into Church Street and turn right at Long Street to reach the tea shop, quite a long way up on the right. From the tea shop, continue up Long Street and turn left into Market Street to return to the car park.

25. Nailsworth and Avening

Length: 6 miles

Summary: A varied circular walk from the village of Avening to the modern garden centre just outside Nailsworth. Mostly on field paths and farm roadways but there is a short distance on the B4014 roadside. Some mud and one moderate ascent through Hazel Wood.

Car Parking: Find a roadside space in Avening. Specimen grid reference 880980. Public conveniences are available at the Drill Hall.

Map: Ordnance Survey Landranger no. 162, Gloucester and the Forest of Dean area.

Tea Shop

The café at The Waterside Garden World is under the same ownership as the well-known Tubby's Tea Shop in Nailsworth and the spacious building is in character with the "glass house" garden centre.

The seating is varied and ranges from low coffee tables and comfy cane chairs to smart dining tables. As might be expected there are many plants around, whilst from the windows there are pleasing views of the surrounding countryside including the remaining chimney of one of the mills in the valley. Very thoughtfully, daily newspapers are provided, adding to the pleasantly unhurried atmosphere.

Although the food counter and refrigerated displays encourage one to forget calorie counts, there is so much variety that one can also be very health conscious in choosing food here.

Breakfast is served until 11am followed by lunches but most items are available all day. Afternoon tea includes cakes, scones, toasted tea cakes, etc. To drink, choose from a range of speciality teas, coffee, elderflower presse, cider, and milk shakes with ice cream.

Description

Situated well up one of the partly industrial valleys which centre on Nailsworth, Avening is by no means a showpiece village. Like all Cotswold villages, it does have some good buildings, particularly the church, with fine Norman work in the north doorway, the low arched north arcade, the base of the tower, and the vaulted chancel roof. Built

Garden Centre and Tea Shop, near Nailsworth

into the wall are carved panels from a previous font, probably dating from the original construction of the church. It is claimed that the wife of William the Conqueror worshipped at the opening service of the church. Should this legend be true, then the church is very early Norman indeed! The Bell Inn and the post office/stores are useful facilities in the village.

Close to Avening are the royal residence of Gatcombe Park and an ancient standing stone – the Tingle Stone.

The "Waterside – A World of Gardening" is an interesting complex, comprehensive and in the modern garden centre image.

Although Nailsworth itself is not included in the circuit, it can readily be added. Despite its situation at a junction of busy roads, and its industrial development, firstly as one of the great manufacturing centres of the later centuries of the Cotswold wool trade, when the valleys around Stroud bustled with mill-based activity and, subsequently, as a mixed industrial/commercial centre following the decline of that trade, Nailsworth still has some interest for the visitor.

Steep, narrow streets, a few surviving weavers' cottages, large converted mills and a great copper kettle are all there, among the considerable array of modern shops and facilities. St George's church is turn of the century, with a large modern mural as its main feature of interest.

The Walk

Start up the minor road by the side of the Bell Inn. This is, (very unusually!), recommended in preference to a footpath below on the right, as this road provides a delightful walking route across pleasant countryside. At first the road climbs quite steeply. Keep right at a junction and pass a second junction.

Descend a little to cross a stream and then stay with the surfaced road to climb steadily past the large Brandhouse Farm, reaching summit level, an open expanse of grassland, soon after the farm. Continue along the same track, now unsurfaced, to and through a plantation. Go through a farm gate at the end (bridleway and footpath signs) and along a defined path across the grass, heading for more woodland, with Nailsworth very much in view, ahead.

After another farm gate continue the gentle descent along the top of a wooded scarp, then along a gully-like path across a meadow. The track becomes a lane then, immediately before a farm gate, turn right at a footpath sign.

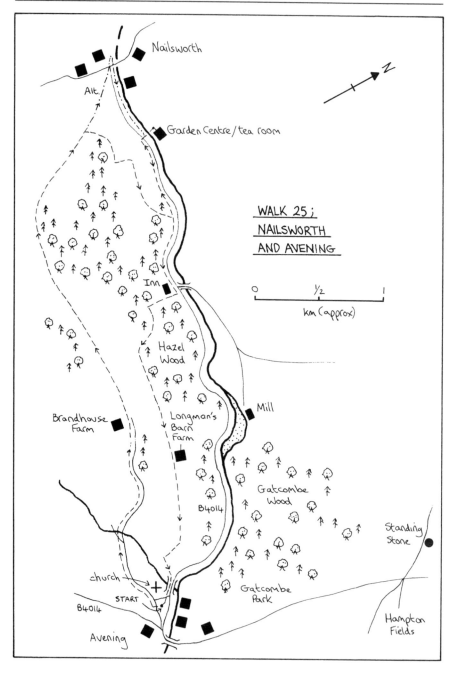

WALK 25;
NAILSWORTH
AND AVENING

From this point to go straight on would lead into Nailsworth in a quarter of a mile.

A minor path forks within a few yards. Keep left to a stile and follow a good path along the bottom edge of woodland. The garden centre destination can now be seen on the far side of a former tipping site. Cross a stream on a railway sleeper bridge, take a stile on the left and carry on, soon with a view of an elegant traditional mill chimney, now surrounded by more prosaic modern industrial buildings.

The path is always evident, as it leads to a stile before descending through a farm gate to the public road. Turn left for about a quarter of a mile to reach the garden centre and Tubby's tea room.

Return along the access road to the B4014 and turn left to retrace part of the outward route. Go a little further along the road to the Weighbridge Inn, with a nice old multi-arched bridge on the left and a road junction. Forty yards past the road junction turn right through a gate with a bridleway sign and commence the considerable ascent of the valley side, initially on a rough, stony path which does double duty as a stream.

Continue to a small gate and enter woodland, following a well-used track still climbing steeply through the trees. At a junction with a wide forestry roadway, turn left, soon on to level ground and even slightly downhill. At the next fork go right, uphill, to a junction with a narrower track Turn left to proceed to a farm gate at the edge of the wood.

Go through and follow a grassy terraced track, slightly downhill, towards Longman's Barn Farm. This open section has splendid views which include Minchinhampton on its hilltop opposite. Pass the farm, with plenty of mud in wet weather, to a gate, and then keep the same line across meadows. A lone gate post surviving from a long defunct wall is a useful guide here, in the absence of a defined path on the ground.

Aim for another farm gate, followed by a path between hedges, which becomes Woodstock Lane, leading straight into Avening village, reaching the main road by the filling station.

26. Minchinhampton and Brimscombe

Length: 5 miles

Summary: Very much an up and down walk. Up, at quite a steep gradient, to the lovely little town of Minchinhampton, then back down to Brimscombe, with some level walking at both top and bottom of the circuit. Fine views from Minchinhampton common and industrial history interest in the Golden Valley at Brimscombe. Some roadside walking across the common.

Car Parking: Spacious roadside layby on the A419 at the Stroud end of Brimscombe. Grid reference 867025.

Map: Ordnance Survey Landranger no. 162, Gloucester and the Forest of Dean area.

Tea Shop

"The Coffee Bean" in Minchinhampton is just so English – in the best possible way. At lunchtime the café was full of regulars, all addressed by name and served by thoughtful, sensible waitresses. The furniture is dark oak, the ceiling beamed. Somewhat out of character, but very functional, there is a large bay window overlooking the main street.

A two course set lunch is available at a very reasonable price but it is also possible to have a healthier option such as a salad, an omelette, or a toasted sandwich. Afternoon teas include scones, bread and butter, jam, cream and cakes. Good quality coffee and tea, including lemon tea, are available all day.

Open 10am to 5pm but closed on Saturday afternoon, Sunday and Monday; also closed during Christmas and New Year period. Tel. 01453 883382.

Description

In medieval times Minchinhampton became a busy little market town. With sheep grazing the great expanse of its high plateau, prosperity up to the 18th century was securely founded on the woollen trade, linked to the water powered mills along the streams in the valleys to the north and south. The 19th century saw the concentration of the trade in those

Minchinhampton

increasingly industrial valleys, focused on nearby Stroud, leaving Minchinhampton as a charming backwater, very much as we see it today.

Harmonious stone buildings cluster round the 17th century market house, with the Church of the Holy Trinity sitting solidly above. The church is noted for its odd, truncated, spire and outstanding 14th century south transept.

Most of the top of the Minchinhampton plateau is common land, 580 acres in the care of the National Trust, after Cleeve (walk no. 2) the second largest in the Cotswolds. Here, there is clear evidence of much earlier occupation. The "Bulwarks" comprises a long iron age bank and a ditch cut into solid rock which, combined with the natural defensive scarp fringing part of the plateau, enclosed approximately 600 acres. Nowadays, the common is criss crossed by roads and much frequented by horses and golfers.

Brimscombe is certainly not pretty, but those who care about industrial history will, with some imagination, find a great deal of interest in that part of the walk along the valley bottom. Firstly, the Thames and Severn Canal, more fully described in walk no. 20, and with its headquarters at "Brimscombe Port", served the numerous mills of the so-called Golden Valley. Then, for some distance following much the same line, came the Great Western Railway, still operational, with passenger services between London, Swindon, Gloucester and Cheltenham.

The Walk

From the layby cross the main road and immediately turn right towards Minchinhampton (signpost). In 40 yards turn left to take a roadway through modern industrial buildings. There is a footpath sign sited on the opposite side of the public road. This may not be the most scenic of footpaths but, with nostalgic imagination, it might be possible to conjure up visions of the great days of the woollen industry in this area. No doubt the fine stone mills were grimy and smelly, obliterating much of the surrounding countryside with plumes of dense smoke!

A modern building to the left of the route has a blue plaque recording "Site of Brimscombe Port, Headquarters of the Thames and Severn Canal Co. Incorporated 1783. Here were offices, warehouses, canal basin and weigh bridge. An important transport centre for over a century". Bear right, along the side of the water, with the fine stone Port Mill still showing some of the relics of its water powered past.

Don't cross a bridge to the right, but continue along the roadway on the nearside of the water. As this terminates, take the obvious footpath, leading to a brick bridge over the canal, by the side of Bourne Mill and the remains of a lock. Pass under the railway and follow what was the canal towpath, between more modern industry, but with steep green slopes now beckoning ahead, as far as a minor road. Perhaps in a hundred years or so, our successors will walk along this route, thinking with nostalgic regret of the demise of English Plastics and all the others which now provide the industry in this historic area. At least, the demolition of the 20th century structures won't be much of a job!

Turn right, cross the River Frome, and fork into Knapp Lane to start the long climb to Minchinhampton. In 10 yards turn right at a set back footpath sign, and go over a stile to ascend gently, with a fence and woodland immediately on the left. The track, muddy in part, is just about visible on the ground. As clumps of bramble are passed, the gradient steepens and a stile with yellow arrow is reached. More open country and the steepest part of the climb follow. The most used route up the grass seems to be close to the woodland on the left. As the gradient eases, there are houses visible both to the left and the right. Keep these roughly equidistant and then aim for a stile/gate by the corner of a third house.

Go left, then right in 20 yards, up a grassy bank and across a minor road to a stile apparent on the skyline. From here a fenced path passes a substantial detached house. The climb is now over and that well-earned pot of tea is only minutes away. Go over two stiles in quick

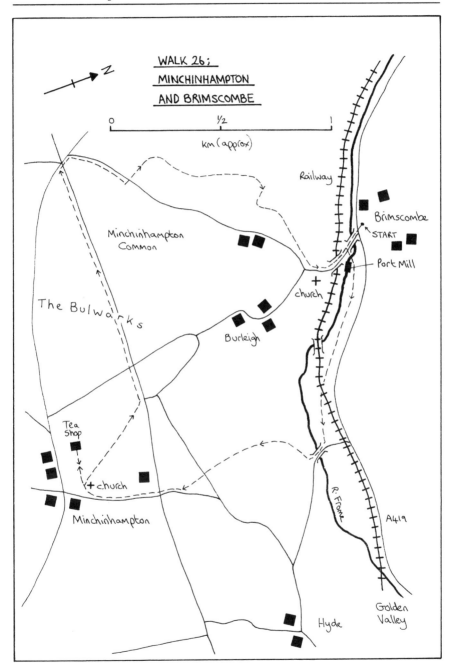

WALK 26;
MINCHINHAMPTON
AND BRIMSCOMBE

0 ½ 1
km (approx)

Railway

Minchinhampton
Common

Brimscombe
START
Port Mill

The Bulwarks

church

Burleigh

Tea
Shop

church

Minchinhampton

R. Frome

A419

Hyde

Golden
Valley

succession and continue the same line towards the evident built-up area.

Yet another stile gives access to a surfaced lane, the Knapp. Turn right, cross the main road and follow Butt Street to the Market Square. The tea shop is about 100 yards along High Street, on the right.

After refreshment and exploration of Minchinhampton, return to the Market Place and turn left to the church, then right to reach the edge of the common. Follow a private road to the left and, as this peters out, continue the same line to reach a cross roads, where Dr. Brown's Road joins the main road along the common. Turn left and stay beside the main road, crossing the Bulwarks, as far as a major junction where no fewer than six roads converge by Tom Long's Post, which marks the point where the notorious highwayman was hanged and buried. There are long views to the right over the valley of the River Frome (Golden Valley).

Turn right to descend beside the Brimscombe road, as far as the first houses on the left. Turn left at a track on the nearside of the houses, and carry on beyond the last house, which has a little tower and a surrounding stone wall. Turn right here, over the grass; there is a just discernible path leading down to a roadway. Join the roadway and continue the descent towards Brimscombe.

As the road rakes back sharp right, go straight ahead over a surfaced track for 10 yards, then descend steeply on a minor path leading to a stile, then pass close to the side of a house. Concrete steps, with handrail, lead to a surfaced road. Turn left, still quite steeply downhill, but soon reaching the bottom of the valley. Go straight ahead at a junction, to ascend to the Minchinhampton – Brimscombe road. Turn left to descend to Brimscombe and return past the Ship Inn to the parking layby.

27. Painswick and Painswick Hill

Length: 6 miles

Summary: A long, but very easy, ascent from Painswick to the splendid summit of Painswick Hill (or Beacon) with a return along the Painswick valley, using a great variety of footpaths, mostly very good, with a small amount of minor road.

Car Parking: Free car park, with public conveniences, a little way south of the church in Painswick. Grid reference 866096.

Map: Ordnance Survey Landranger no. 162, Gloucester and the Forest of Dean.

Tea Shop

St Michael's is an "Olde Worlde" tea shop, part of a tall, typically Cotswold building, very close to Painswick church. It proved to be particularly welcoming on a dismal Friday afternoon in December. Open for morning coffee, lunches, afternoon teas and even dinner by arrangement, St Michael's is also a guest house with bed and breakfast available.

The decor is very harmonious with pine furniture and blue and white matching pottery.

According to the time of day, the menu is varied but please note that there is a modest minimum charge from noon onwards. Cream teas, with a selection of delicious cakes made by the owners, are a speciality – a particularly popular favourite being the proprietor's own recipe apricot cake.

Open daily 10am – 5pm (but like many privately owned tea shops, could close early if custom is quiet). Closed on Mondays except Bank Holidays. Tel. 01452 812998.

Description

Painswick – the "Queen of the Cotswolds" – is without doubt one of the most attractive small towns in the district. A jumble of buildings of light grey stone, intersected by twisting, narrow, sloping streets, bears wit-

Painswick Post Office

ness to the prosperity of the 17th and 18th centuries, brought about by the local cloth making industry, although some surviving houses are older than this.

The 15th century church still carries the marks of shot fired during the Civil War and its peal of twelve bells is renowned. The large number of bells is said to result from local determination not to be outdone by nearby Stroud, where the more usual peal of eight bells was increased to ten. The churchyard is famous for its great collection of table tombstones, designed and carved by a local family of masons and for the yew trees, allegedly ninety-nine in number. This number is subject to two legends; one states that attempts to plant a hundredth tree have always been frustrated by the Devil, as the tree has never survived; the other claims that it is impossible to count the number of individual trees. Some of the yews were planted more than 200 years ago but the majority are of the 19th century. The impressive lych gate was constructed partially with re-used timbers from the church belfry, with decorations including musical notation. At the south end of the churchyard are the former town stocks, with the fine 17th century Court House nearby.

Modern amenities in Painswick include a range of shops, inns, tea shops and a Tourist Information Centre. The fine viewpoint of Painswick Hill (or "Beacon") at 283m (929 feet) is crowned by the ramparts of an iron age fort. The adjacent expanse of open land is largely used as a golf course, across which there are many rights of way.

One mile to the north of the town is the Rococo Garden, six acres adjacent to Painswick House, said to be the only surviving example of this once popular gardening style. The garden and refreshment room are open to the public from January to November, Wednesdays to Sundays and Bank Holidays.

The Walk

From the car park go north along the main street. This is New Street, "New" referring to 1260 in this case! At the cross roads, turn left into Gloucester Street, rising gently. At a road junction by a telephone box keep straight on, with open country now on the left, behind a long stone wall and a row of trees.

Pass the end of Gyde Road, then turn right into Golf Course Road, with a Cotswold Way signpost. In less than 100 yards fork left on to an unmade track, opposite the gates of a covered reservoir. In about 100 yards turn left at a gap in the fence, marked "walkers only", cross a track in a depression and ascend rudimentary steps on the far side. A well-defined woodland path now continues the steady ascent. Ignore any paths to left or right and emerge from the woodland at a very minor road, signposted "Cemetery; Sheepscombe".

Turn right, descending slightly, to reach a part of the golf course and then turn left at a post with yellow arrow to head for the left hand corner of the cemetery wall ahead. Go straight on, as indicated by a yellow arrow on a post, soon crossing a steeply rising fairway to another post with arrow at the edge of woodland on the far side.

A good track traverses the woodland, reaching an unmade roadway by the former Catsbrain quarry, now a depot for architectural salvage and garden materials. Go straight ahead to pass a road barrier and join a minor road. Turn left up the road for 40 yards and then turn right at the side of a golf tee. The track forks at once, the Cotswold Way to the right, and our route to Painswick Hill to the left, along the rim above an area of disturbed ground, presumably historic quarrying activity.

When passage is safe from flying golf balls, ascend to the summit of the hill, crossing the well-defined defences of the hill fort, most impressive on the west, where there has been least disturbance. The extensive and interesting views include the city of Gloucester.

Continue along the top, turning to the right to drop a little to a broad, well-used, track along the top of Pope's Wood, with the golf course on

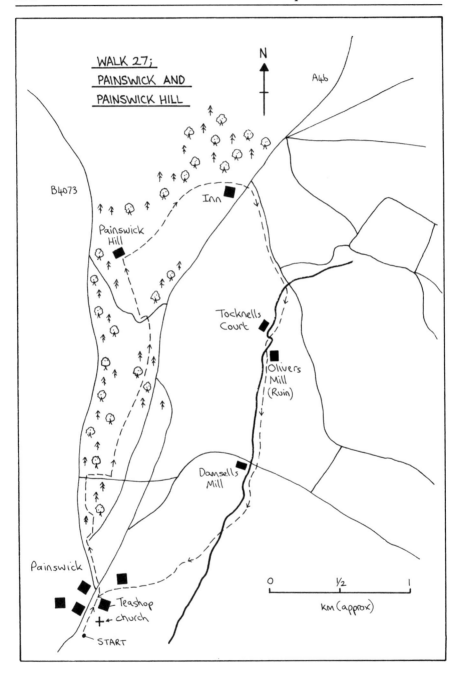

WALK 27;
PAINSWICK AND
PAINSWICK HILL

N

A46

B4073

Inn

Painswick
Hill

Tocknells
Court

Olivers
Mill
(Ruin)

Damsells
Mill

Painswick

Teashop
church

START

0   ½   1

km (approx)

the right. The Cotswold Way joins on the right as the A46 road is approached, passing the entrances to two nature reserves on the left, Pope's Wood and Buckholt Wood, and following a surfaced road down to the Royal William Inn, on the main road.

Cross the A46, turning left for 50 yards or so, then right to take a descending bridleway leading to a minor road. Turn right, downhill. At a road fork, bear right, signposted "Sheepscombe", to descend to the valley bottom. Turn right, by the side of the stream along a private drive leading to Tocknell's Court, a beautiful old house. Cross the stream to a green track on the far side running parallel to the stream and the driveway.

By a small pond in the stream, go over a stile and continue along the lower edge of a meadow to a gate. Pass a cottage and, as the path forks, turn left through the ruins of Oliver's Mill. Cross the stream and bear right to a stile. The path continues along the valley bottom to Damsell's Mill, over several stiles with the stream now on the right.

The Mill is now a private house, but it is claimed that the old water wheel is still in situ, below the building. The track continues, to the left of the mill, waymarked with yellow arrow, along the side of the stream, now in a deep, glen-like ravine, well-wooded with oak and beech.

Cross a wide bridge over the stream, likely to be muddy, and choose the left of the three routes offered by arrows on a post, close to the hedge and fence on the left. After 150 yards, reach a double gate and stile by Highgrove (no – not the home of the Prince of Wales!). On the left is a curious circular ruin and what appears to be a dried out mill pond.

At a gate/stile with blue arrow, go over and follow the unsurfaced Highgrove access road back to Painswick, climbing a little through open country. Painswick is entered by Vicarage Street, a long approach lined by a rich array of diverse buildings, so typical of the town. Bear left, then right, towards the church, to find St Michael's tea shop facing the churchyard on the north side.

28. Prinknash and Cooper's Hill

Length: 4 miles

Summary: This walk packs a great deal into its modest length. A "cheese-rolling" hill; Nature Reserve; woodland; monastic park land; a modern abbey with its various attractions, are all included. Inevitably, there is a fair amount of ascent; but the paths are generally very good.

Car Parking: Small car park at the foot of Cooper's Hill, part sloping and with roughish surface. Grid reference 893147. Accessed by cul de sac road off the A46, signposted "Cooper's Hill".

Map: Ordnance Survey Landranger nos. 162, Gloucester and the Forest of Dean area (85%); 163, Cheltenham and Cirencester area (15%).

Tea Shop

Sorry to say, there is no atmosphere of a monastic refectory in this large tea room at Prinknash. Indeed it is well away from the abbey, adjacent to the other visitor facilities including the viewing gallery of the pottery. From the café, doors open onto a long patio with tables and sun umbrellas.

The counter display of food gives a choice of salads, sandwiches, etc. with soup, sausages, chips, and other hot foods available to order. During the afternoon, scones, cakes, toasted tea-cakes, may be more tempting than the hot dishes but the whole range is served all day.

Open 9am – 4.45pm seven days each week all the year; closed only on Christmas Day, Boxing Day and Good Friday. Tel. 01452 812239.

Description

Cooper's Hill is situated at the northern end of a high spur jutting out from the western edge of the Cotswolds, quite close to the city of Gloucester. It would hardly merit attention if it were not for the annual Whitsuntide cheese-rolling competition, at which large circular cheeses are rolled down the hill, pursued by the (foolhardy?) competitors. Anyone catching a cheese keeps it. Looking at the gradient it is no surprise that few cheeses are caught and that injuries are frequent.

Most of the hilltop comprises a Nature Reserve, itself within a larger area classified as a Site of Special Scientific Interest.

Prinknash Abbey

At least initially, Prinknash ("Prinish") Abbey may come as something of a disappointment. Preconceptions of romantic ruins of great medieval buildings hardly prepare one for a first view of this prosaic, no-nonsense structure, entirely typical of its date of 1972. Could it not grace the North Circular Road or Great Western Avenue? However, the Abbey is built of real Cotswold stone, quarried at Guiting, and certainly does occupy a wonderful site. Perhaps the kindly passage of time will soften the present harsh appearance.

The Abbey community is of the Benedictine Order, the monks originally moving to Prinknash earlier this century, when they occupied an old Cotswold manor house half a mile from the present Abbey. Public access is limited to the Abbey church, plainly furnished by the craft work of the monks, incorporated into the rear part of the main building.

Beds of clay discovered when the foundations were being excavated led to the establishment of Prinknash Pottery, initially being worked by the monks themselves, but now a thriving local industry providing financial support for the Abbey. Housed in the same building as the gift shops and tea room, the pottery is open to visitors for viewing during normal working hours.

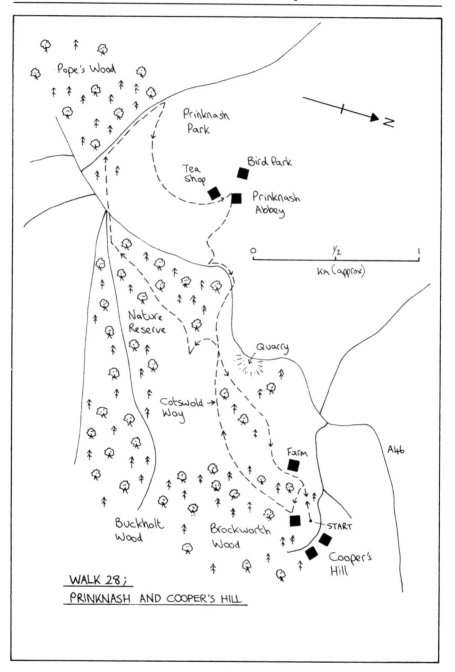

WALK 28;
PRINKNASH AND COOPER'S HILL

A little way further down the hill, Prinknash Bird Park is a beautiful park with lakes and woodland, deer, pygmy goats, fish and a colourful collection of unusual birds (open daily to visitors throughout the year).

The Walk

Start along the track signposted "Cotswold Way to Painswick", entering the Cooper's Hill Nature Reserve at a kissing gate and rising quite steeply through the woods above the little hamlet of Cooper's Hill. After a short level section turn left, uphill, at a fork with a yellow arrow and white dot (Cotswold Way way mark) on a tree ahead. A sharp climb leads to the maypole on the hill top above the car park, launching point for the cheeses.

Turn right here, following the lower of two tracks back to the woods, soon gently downhill. At a junction take the second track on the left (yellow arrow, white dot), on the level. Bear right at another junction then, at a stile, follow the arrow, left, to descend along the edge of woodland, almost at once reaching a fork.

Either way will do here, keeping broadly the same line through attractive mixed woodland, with the A46 road not far below. At the next junction go straight ahead, rising, and still with the Cotswold Way waymark, soon climbing quite steeply. Pass a Buckholt Wood National Nature Reserve sign with some useful information.

After the sign bear right, now downhill along yet another very good track. Pass an N.N.R. information board for Rough Park Wood, as a minor road angles in from the left. Turn right, along the roadside, towards its junction with the main road. Cross the main road diagonally to a Cotswold Way finger post and follow the obvious path through the woodland to another minor road.

Turn right, downhill. As the top of a steep descent is reached, the views over Gloucester open up for the first time. A few yards down the slope turn right along a private roadway leading through the Prinknash Estate. The Abbey itself is soon glimpsed through the trees, across a valley, but the roadway winds around to follow the contours, passing St Peter's Grange on the way. This is a fine old Cotswold building, with numerous extensions and additions giving a quite indeterminable shape to the present structure.

The utilitarian building which houses pottery, gift shops and tea shop is next, with the entrance to the Bird Park below. Access to the Abbey church, with its appealing simplicity, is round the far end of the main building.

Ascend the Abbey approach road and turn left at the main road. The splendid view compensates for any traffic nuisance as the road is followed for a short distance. Immediately after a sharp right hand bend cross the road and take a wide, unsurfaced, unsignposted roadway, rising into the woodland. Pass a "Cooper's Hill Local Nature Reserve" sign with yellow arrow and keep left at a fork, to join the outward route (Cotswold Way) for a short distance.

At the next fork, where the Cotswold Way goes right, go left, descending slightly, with a fence fairly close on the left. Keep descending and, at the next fork, go right, to approach an open field. Bear right here. A minor but well-defined path heads for a farm, passing above a solitary house.

The farm house and outbuildings show evidence of several stages of construction/renovation over the centuries, including some half timbered work. Approximately 100 yards beyond the farm, slant right, passing a "Cooper's Hill Local Nature Reserve" board, and climb steeply for a short distance to rejoin the outward route again. Turn left to return steeply downhill to the car park.

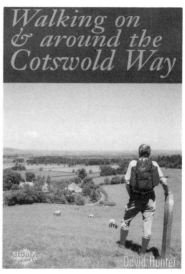

 MAGAZINE

 EVENTS

Tea is our most social and sociable drink – a part of our national heritage and daily life for well over 300 years. The Tea Club exists so its members can share and enjoy the history, traditions and romance associated with this fascinating drink.

 COMPETITIONS

 MEMBER DISCOUNTS

 TASTINGS & SAMPLING

 A FREE GIFT WHEN YOU JOIN

THERE'S SO MUCH MORE
TO TEA THAN JUST
A CUPPA !

HOW TO JOIN

Simply send your name, full address and postcode to:

The Tea Club
PO Box 221
Guildford, Surrey GU1 3YT

and an application form will be sent to you immediately.

Tea Club Memberships are also a great gift idea – why not send one to a friend !